Four hours with Marcia Wieder brought back the meaning of life! Weeks later, our team was still buzzing. You can be assured we will call upon you again.

—AT&T

We came away from your inspirational presentation unstoppable in accomplishing our goals.

—Young Presidents' Organization

Marvelous! Fantastic! Superb! Only superlatives are appropriate to describe you and your process. We want you back.

—National Association of Professional Saleswomen

Everything they said about you was true. You are a dynamo in front of a group, and your energy and enthusiasm demonstrate your strong belief and commitment to your subject.

—*USA Today*

It is clear that you understood our needs and were able to relate them effectively. We look forward to future opportunities together.

—U.S. State Department

* * *

Making Your Dreams Come True moves you from inner excellence to outer manifestation.

—Carol Orsborn, Author of *Enough is Enough* and *Inner Excellence*

Forget wishing on stars and rainbows—*Making Your Dreams Come True* shows how you can make your dreams come true.

—Rieva Lesonsky, Editor-in-chief, *Entrepreneur* magazine

Often the biggest barriers we face in life are self-imposed. *Making Your Dreams Come True* can help dismantle those barriers and propel you onward to a life of fulfillment and adventure.

—David Pease, Author of *The Strength to Strive* and former Business Manager—Miami Dolphins

A new consulting business of dream architects to help people implement their dreams will show up in the '90's.

—Faith Popcorn, Author *The Popcorn Report: On The Future of Your Company, Your World, Your Life*

Marcia Wieder is full of practical ideas, entertainingly presented in a manner which helps you take charge of your life.

—Patricia Fripp, Former President, National Speakers Association

Making Your Dreams Come True shows you that anything worth having is worth striving for with all your might.

—Orville Redenbacher, Popcorn king

This book is the catalyst for everyone to start down the path to make their dreams become a reality. The difference between having a dream and making a dream come true is right now at your fingertips, thanks to Marcia Wieder!

—Kathy Smith, Fitness expert

The result from working with Marcia's book is health, happiness, and peace. Success is a given.

—Hal Uplinger, Co-producer, *Live Aid* Telecast

It's powerful and it's insightful. It penetrates the most critical element of success for a business. It's a magical, but practical, journey into the most obvious leverage point of a corporation, its people.

—Richard Falcone, Vice President—Sales, AT&T

Making Your Dreams Come True acts as the wake-up call we all need. The techniques helped me move quickly and powerfully, during a very busy time, and the "Real People" stories were a "silver lining."

—Grace McGartland, former President, National Association of Women Business Owners

We too often misplace our purpose in living our lives. The basis of Marcia Wieder's approach is essential for anyone committed to living life to the fullest.

—Jonathan Clarke, 2000/Love: The Tennis Celebration to End World Hunger

I have literally seen miracles happen when clients develop the self-confidence to follow their dreams. This book helps guide you in following your own dreams, so that you can be the best at whatever you do.

—Dr. Lillian Glass, Author of *Talk to Win* and *He Says/She Says*

Don't let weeds grow around your dreams.

—H. Jackson Brown, Jr., Author of *Life's Little Instruction Book, Vol. II*

Marcia Wieder not only inspires but actually shows you how to ignite your passion and use it to make your personal and professional dreams a reality.

—John Gray Ph.D., Author of the national bestseller, *Men Are from Mars, Women Are from Venus*

Your job is to dream the perfect life. Marcia shows you how to make that dream come true—step by practical step. You *must* read this book.

—Patricia Aburdene, Co-Author of *Megatrends for Women* and *Megatrends 2000*

MARCIA WIEDER
"Making Your Dreams Come True" Consultant

Marcia Wieder has coached hundreds of corporations and individuals in the fine art of manifestation. Whether the dream is creating a company that works, building a winning team, or bringing more passion to the workplace, Marcia is guaranteed to get people in action.

The core message in all of Marcia's work is her quotable quote, "Passion is the access to power." She is a terrific example of a woman who is living a dream-come-true life, fueled with passion and producing results. Currently, she is happily living near the water in San Francisco, California.

SPEAKER Marcia's speeches are refreshing in how they blend brand-new information with ideas that are thousands of years old. Her energetic presentations are filled with practical, usable tips and techniques for creating what we want. Participants say her speeches are insightful and inspirational. She has even presented her workshop material recently on "Oprah."

TRAINER Marcia's favorite audiences are business people who allow her to be both creative and strategic when working with them. During her workshops, she produces dynamic results with corporate clients worldwide and is often described as a "firecracker."

ENTREPRENEUR For over ten years, Marcia has been a business owner. She has always had a talent for packaging and marketing unique concepts. As the Dreams Come True Consultant, she has developed the ultimate "how to," how to have anything!

AUTHOR Marcia has taken her three easy steps for having anything, added to them her "Passion Pyramid," and done what hundreds of people have asked her to do: she wrote *Making Your Dreams Come True*. It is a straightforward marketing approach, guaranteed to get readers moving on any personal or professional dream.

Marcia has two big personal dreams that she is currently "in action" on. The first is to change the way people think about and speak about their dreams, from "maybe someday" to "when." She is currently creating a line of products to help people do this. (See the order form for the Making Your Dreams Come True Cards in the back of this book.)

Her second big dream is to travel the world speaking about something that will have a positive impact on people. She created a partnership with the World Association of Women Entrepreneurs, who are supporting her by presenting her workshop and this book in thirty countries.

MAKING YOUR
DREAMS
COME TRUE

A Plan for Easily Discovering
and Achieving the Life You Want!

MARCIA WIEDER

MASTERMEDIA LIMITED
New York

Library of Congress Cataloging-in-Publication Data

Wieder, Marcia.
   Making your dreams come true: a plan for easily discovering and
achieving the life you want / Marcia Wieder.
      p.   cm.
   ISBN 0-942361-78-4 (pbk.): $9.95
   1. Success—Psychological aspects.   I. Title.
BF637.S8W512 1993
158′.1—dc20   93-19035
                                                            CIP

Manufactured in the United States of America
Production services by Martin Cook Associates, New York
10 9 8 7 6 5 4 3

CONTENTS

For All Who Dare to Dream—
especially
Mom & Dad

A C K N O W L E D G M E N T S

Thank you, Lorrie Caplan-Shern, for being there every day, for being my best friend, and for reminding me that I can do anything. And thank you, Stephen Shern, for sharing Lorrie.

Thanks to Joy and Scott Wieder for your love and creativity. I am lucky to have you both as partners.

Thank you to Grace McGartland and Virginia Littlejohn. You are both inspirational creative forces in my life. You make me play a bigger game.

Thank you, Lisa Berlin, for the magic you bring to my life and to so many other people's lives too.

Thank you, David Avery, for seeing me as bigger than I see myself.

Thanks to Stacy Howlin Clarke and Rhea Blanken for being powerful coaches.

Thank you to Jeff Davidson for lending your know-how and shortcutting the process, to Karen Heller for making everything look so polished, and to Susan Stautberg for publishing this.

Thank you, Gillian Rudd and Anselm Rothschild, for being angels on my shoulder and showing me how to create heaven on earth.

And thank you, Kevin Zmarthie, for being a dear friend and loving me no matter what.

F O R E W O R D

What if you could create what you want by being able to close the gap between dreams and reality? In person and now in *Making Your Dreams Come True*, Marcia Wieder shows people how to close the gap.

As a professional speaker, Marcia's spirit and style fill any room. She produces powerful results with her corporate clients and business associates worldwide. In describing what Marcia's system does for them, clients have commented that she produces extraordinary results and reignites passion in the audience. After engaging with Marcia, people who claim to have forgotten their dream remember and "get going" on that dream.

I first met Marcia shortly after reading material by Richard Bach, Jane Roberts, and Dennis Waitley, among others. These writings profoundly changed my life, and when I realized they could change anyone's life, I felt compelled to share this joy with everyone with whom I came in contact. I met Marcia just then. Coincidence #1.

Our career paths took us in different directions, and we lost contact for some time. Marcia called me and asked me to read *Making Your Dreams Come True*, and to write this foreword, at the precise moment when I was in the process of rediscovering my own true purpose and my life was again beginning to take an exciting new direction. I felt the joy of the knowledge and wisdom contained in this book, and the compulsion to help share it with everyone. Coincidence #2.

It is said that when the student is ready, the teacher will appear—and vice versa. The fact that you are reading this book is no accident. Coincidence #3.

Call it coincidence, or synchronicity, or magic. It is part of the power that surrounds us, is within us, and is available to us when we recognize true beliefs about ourselves and our passions, cultivate them, and allow, with joy, our inner voices and teachings into our everyday lives.

There are many paths to the truth. In this book, Marcia Wieder has been able to garner truths from many sources, metaphysical, spiritual, and literary, and has uniquely combined this knowledge in a practical and pragmatic guide to self-discovery, or better yet, rediscovery. This book provides a real basis for applying these truths, and gives us an imaginative action plan placing us on the path to realizing our greatest dreams.

I have rediscovered that I have always been at my happiest, and most successful, when working with the things I love, that are exciting to me, that I feel passionate about, and in which I feel destined to make a contribution. For me these things have always involved music, show business, and electronics. From my days as an NBC page through all my various career experiences, from commercial producer for Johnny Carson to program executive in charge of the original *Saturday Night Live* to becoming an Emmy award-winning producer, I have always been most successful when surrounded by, or in close proximity to, the elements of my passion. It is when one gets off the track, following the money instead of the heart, that things will always take a turn for the worse.

Marianne Williamson reminds us that all of our choices are made either out of love or out of fear. *Making Your Dreams Come True* also speaks to this basic truth. If you are passionate, love what you do, and spread that love through what you do, the possibilities are limitless.

You are about to embark on an exciting journey in a realm that you perhaps thought you couldn't do much about—making your dreams come true. Bring your hopes and highest aspirations, because *Making Your Dreams Come True* is going to show you how to make them a part of your everyday existence. I'm excited for you!

—Richard S. Traum

You've got to have a dream if you
want to make a dream come true.
—Rodgers and Hammerstein

P R E F A C E

My life is a dream come true. In all areas of my life I'm living a life I love. This book will show you how to do the same for yourself.

This is a tried and true, tested and proven technology that will take you through a step-by-step process for Making All Your Dreams Come True.

The basic formula is simple:

1. Get clear about what you want to create,
2. Remove the obstacles, especially the limiting beliefs, and
3. Allow the Magic to happen or Design the Strategies for getting there.

The essence of the formula is *passion*. Passion is what compels you to action, turns you on, what makes your life rich and extraordinary. This book will show you how to discover or rediscover what you're passionate about and how to bring it to all areas of your life. How does that sound?

For almost ten years I lived in Washington, D.C., and was president of a multimedia creative services agency, managing fourteen employees. Although successful by many people's standards, I was not passionate about what I was doing, about how I was doing it, about the people with whom I was doing it, and about where I was doing it.

My dream was to be free—free to travel anywhere, anytime. Free to do what I wanted when I wanted, even to have my portable office be wherever I happened to be.

My dream included a magnificent view of water and mountains, clean, fresh air, and a quiet, healthy environment.

My dream included partnering with creative visionaries to make an impact on the world, in addition to traveling the world in style and elegance, speaking about something inspiring.

My dream included having lots of fun, creating my work as play, and living a life filled with full self-expression.

Sound outrageous?

Recently, I picked up and moved to San Francisco. When people ask why, I tell them because of the view and the lifestyle, and that's what matters to me now. Once I was committed, the Magic showed up and I sold my D.C. condominium furnished, for full price, and without a realtor. I climbed into my car and took a few months to visit with friends and family as I made my way west, with my fax machine and portable computer in tow.

I've become a successful Dreams Come True Consultant and speaker. I was paid to travel to Hawaii, among other exotic places, and am scheduled to do a thirty-country speaking tour, inspiring people to go for their dreams.

I've worked with hundreds of people, helping them to get clear about what turns them on, supporting them as they get into action on their dreams and their lives. I look and feel ten years younger, and I'm the healthiest I've ever been. I'm completely free and I'm very happy.

It all begins with a dream. You can make all your dreams come true. It all starts here.

I N T R O D U C T I O N

*A new consulting business of dream architects to help people
implement their dreams will show up in the '90s.*
—*Faith Popcorn,* The Popcorn Report

You are holding in your hands the definitive work on making
your dreams come true, having the life you love, and living a life
filled with passion; in essence, having it all. When you've finished reading this book, you will know how:

- You really want your life to be;
- You can develop a dream that inspires you;
- You can look at your life with a fresh perspective; and
- You can design your environment to implement the tech-
  niques you've learned.

Beginning with the first chapter, you will learn to use language that empowers you to "speak your dream." Possibilities
you never knew existed will emerge, and you will trust the
Magic in the universe to produce extraordinary results in your
everyday life.

Sound enticing?

In every chapter, you will find clarity as well as the action
steps that will prompt you to nod in knowing appreciation. The
pages in this book will offer you methods of achieving everything you want in life. The hands-on exercises presented
throughout will help serve as your personal record of everything
you learned about your dreams and how to accomplish them.
The Making Your Dreams Come True Workbook will walk you
through the process.

This book is written with you as its focus. You can use it as
if it were a highly paid dream architect, taking you by the hand
to lead you through the process of making your dreams come
true. Interact fully with its pages, and when you are done, I
believe you'll say, "I can make my dreams come true any time
I choose."

MAKING YOUR
DREAMS COME TRUE

WHAT IS A DREAM?

Nothing happens unless first a dream.
—Carl Sandburg

Most people think of dreams either as some kind of unattainable fantasy, or as something they do in their sleep. Neither of those definitions is what I mean when I speak of dreams.

I define dreams as the aspirations, desires, goals, and hopes that you most want for yourself. Moreover, these are the kind of dreams you have while you are very much awake.

My formula for Making Your Dreams Come True is simple.

First
Get clear about what your dream is.
Second
Remove the obstacles, especially the limiting beliefs.
Third
Allow the Magic to happen or
Design the Strategies to get there.

It's that simple. That's the formula for having it all—a life you love, and the time and freedom to enjoy it.

Four Key Words

The word "dreams" has long been misinterpreted, as if dreams were like puffy clouds in the sky—beautiful, but unreachable. The dictionary offers a different interpretation not only of "dreams" but also of several other words that I'll be using throughout this process. Therefore, I'll start by defining some terms:

Dream (n.), a fond hope or aspiration; (v.) to conceive of or devise.

Possibility (n.), that which may or can be, that which may or can be done, that which is capable of existing, something that is conceivable.

Magic (n.), producing extraordinary results.

Beliefs (n.), what you hold to be true, your opinions or judgments.

It's interesting that the dictionary describes "dream" as a way to achieve your fond aspirations, which suggests possibility and hope, while most people have a sense of hopelessness and futility about their dreams. Yet, their dreams continue to live as an ember, flickering in the back of their minds. Using this book, you will learn to create clarity about what you want, and to get your dreams out of your head and into your reality.

Many of us regard "possibility" as something that's not *im*-possible, although *Webster's* tells us that possibility is something

ANYTHING IS POSSIBLE.

within the realm of our grasp. I used to believe that anything was possible as long as I could figure out in advance how to do it. Eventually, I realized this was a limiting belief and that I was stopping myself from going for what I wanted, often before I even began. Now I believe that *anything is possible* as long as you believe it. My life is filled with opportunities galore, many that I surely would not have encountered if I were still operating with my old belief.

Indeed, when you open up to the potential of having what you want, you allow extraordinary results—Magic—to appear in your life. "Extraordinary results" are not necessarily mystical, although they may be outside the bounds of what you've already experienced. When you clarify what you're committed to having, and believe that Anything Is Possible, the techniques in this book will seem like Magic and show up magically in your life.

I love the dictionary definition of Magic. It reinforces the concept that much of our lives, when filled with extraordinary results, is a magical experience. Have you written off the Magic in your life as illusionary? Do you think that Magic is kids' stuff?

AT&T, one of America's corporate giants, currently has a campaign for its employees called Ten Million Magical Moments. The telecommunications company knows that the use of Magic, or simply allowing the Magic to happen, produces extraordinary results. AT&T says, and I agree, that it's time to find a new way of speaking, of thinking and doing things. Magic, found in each individual, is one of the methods of choice.

Are you using the Magic? Are you letting it flow in your life? Sometimes, getting out of the way, not controlling every little detail, allows Magic to happen. Remember step three of my formula, "Let the Magic happen."

You can start making your dreams come true today—right now—by being clear about what a dream is, by believing that Anything Is Possible, by allowing the Magic to come into your life and produce extraordinary results.

Your beliefs are what you hold to be true, your opinions and judgments. Ponder this powerful thought: when you can hear your beliefs in your head, you can transform your life. This piece of information is worth its weight in gold and will be repeated and explained in chapter 7.

What Is Your Dream?

In talking to people about what they want, I find that most of them characterize "dreams" in the same way they perceive "fantasy." That is, most people don't believe their dreams will

LIFE CAN BE A MAGICAL EXPERIENCE.

come true unless something miraculous happens: if they win the lottery, if Mr. or Ms. Right comes along, or if their stars are aligned in the heavens. "My dream—maybe someday, but probably not" is the way many of us think about our dreams.

A dream can be exotic or glamorous, but it does not have to be. Your dream can be anything from spending more time with the family to doubling your business. Dreams can range from the mundane to the esoteric, and sometimes what you truly want can come as a complete surprise to you. At the end of this chapter, you will find some "Real People" stories. These anecdotes are used as illustrations throughout the book. They are all true situations and they all demonstrate how the techniques I'll describe can be used in every facet of your life.

To enter into the process of achieving your dream, start with step one, clarifying what you want. Many people think this is an impossible or difficult request and never do it. I recommend you start here. Select one thing in any area of your life that you dream of having. On page 8, there is a place for you to commit your dream to paper. Put into a single sentence the essence of what you're committed to having. Don't worry that you can't define all the details or that you don't believe it's possible. This will come as you move forward. The key is to get in touch with what you feel passionate about, what excites and motivates you.

Think about a time in your life when you spoke to others about an idea, and your idea turned into something more concrete. There is a real power in getting your dream out of your head. Speaking to someone else about it is one of the most powerful things you can do to make it come true. Perhaps the more you talked about your concept, the more real it became. Write down what you want. If you can't formulate your dream yet, make something up. Start someplace and practice. Although it may seem ridiculous now, it will often work to lead you down the right path. When you're ready to write out your

---

IDENTIFYING YOUR DREAM

(Example: I, Diane, will have great success in my new business while balancing my family and social life.)*

I, _____, have the following dream:

_____

_____

_____

*Balance, in some form, is one of the most common dreams people have described when working with me.

---

dream, you can apply the techniques you learn as you move through this book.

What Are Your Expectations?

What do you expect to have when you've finished this book? Perhaps you're looking for a blueprint to get you from where you are to where you want to be. Maybe you're seeking a strategy or tactic that will divide the work of reaching your dreams into specific areas of concentration and give you a step-by-step plan for getting there.

You can turn this book into a real action plan for making your dreams come true by deciding now what you intend to have by the time you've finished reading it.

> # My goal is that you fulfill your dreams as you complete this book.

If that's not your goal too, you may want to put the book down now, and think about why you bought it in the first place.

The process of defining your expectations and getting your dream out of your head and into reality can follow these steps:

- Think about what you want.
- Visualize what you want.
- Write down what you want and read it aloud to yourself.
- Speak about what you want, and share it with others.
- Listen to yourself, and for opportunities in the world to make your dreams come true.
- Be your dream, actually live it.
- Do what you want to do, so that you can have what you want to have.
- Get up and get going. As the TV commercial says, "Just do it."

Start to act the part right now. If your dream is to run a dude ranch, a fun thing you might do is buy boots and a cowboy hat, and enjoy wearing them around the house or with friends. That may be enough for you right now. You may decide that you want to be in greater action toward your dream, or that you want your dream to come true in its entirety by the end of this book. It's all up to you. Have a sense of humor and "play" with it; it doesn't need to be hard work. Enjoy the process.

The techniques await you. Don't sit back to see how it un-
folds; it *won't* happen unless you interact with the process. Let
this book make a difference in your life; use it to pull you
forward so you can get what you want. Start now.

REAL PEOPLE: LARRY

Larry wanted to double his income within the next calendar year
without burning himself out. His goal was reasonable; in fact,
it's done all the time. Larry came to me because he didn't know
how to accomplish it.

I told Larry that we'd start the process of making his dream
come true by getting in touch with what he's passionate about.
Larry balked. "Wait a minute," he said. "I don't want to examine my whole life, I just want to know how to double my
business."

I said, "Larry, you have to trust the process."

What Larry discovered by following my approach was that
having powerful partnerships and intimate relationships had
been driving forces throughout his life; that's what really excited him. Although he "knew" this subconsciously, actually
articulating it gave him a real boost of energy. When he realized
the passion he felt about creating powerful partnerships, Larry
understood that he needed to learn how to develop associations
with anyone at any time that he chose, and that this would be
the secret to his success and help make his financial dream
come true.

As we continued to probe, Larry also became aware that by
holding on to old beliefs that did not serve his needs, he was
limiting his potential to create partnerships. For example, he
had developed the habit of not "revealing his playing cards," he
feared taking the "wrong" kind of people into his confidence,
he worried that others wouldn't uphold their end of a bargain,
or that they didn't have the "right" address or the "best" cre-

> # Trust the process
> # of making your
> # dreams come true.

dentials to be his partner. He eliminated wonderful potential partners before ever giving them a chance. Together, we removed the obstacles, the limiting beliefs that were in Larry's way. You'll have the opportunity to remove your limiting beliefs later in the process. For now, it's powerful to learn to recognize what they are.

Once clear about what made him feel passionate, and with his limiting beliefs out of the way, Larry made a conscious commitment to be able to develop partnerships with anyone at any time that he chose. Now he's excited about living his life, not just about doubling his business. His entire life is quite different.

Passion is the access to power; when Larry got in touch with his passion, he developed the power to take the first step toward his dream. Now he has more than two dozen strategic partnerships with associates, friends, agents, even competitors, all of whom are helping him achieve his goal of doubling his business. Larry understands at last how critical passion is as a component in the formula for success.

REAL PEOPLE: NANCY

Nancy had been successful on Wall Street, making a six-figure salary. Now she was starting a whole new life: she was simultaneously pregnant with her first child and leaving the world of

GET IN TOUCH WITH YOUR PASSION.

stocks and bonds to start a new business. She was absolutely committed to her dream of having quality personal time with her friends and family, while developing and building the new business. She was determined to have a balanced life.

A successful person is often also an overcommitted person, and Nancy fit the description. She was aware that she had designed so much into her life that there wasn't room to create anything new. Therefore, we began by cleaning out the clutter. We moved things out of the way, consolidated, organized, and created space, not just physically but emotionally, mentally, and spiritually. Finally, Nancy had *room* to design a whole new future, and she began to live her dream by making deliberate choices, not merely responding to whatever life threw her way.

Then we designed the strategies for her to achieve her dream. There were specific marketing and sales techniques for growing the business, but there were also strategies for enjoying her pregnancy and having quality time with her husband. Wherever possible, we doubled up on strategies, to allow Nancy more time. For example, one tactic that permitted Nancy simultaneously to enjoy her pregnancy and to have quality time with her mate was to take a daily walk with her husband. Later, we turned this technique into a project with the goal of walking two hundred miles before the baby was born. This project supported Nancy's needs for a healthy body and baby, for exercise and relaxation, and for time with her spouse. You'll learn more about projects, strategies, and tactics as you read on.

REAL PEOPLE: CAROL

Carol was once a professional dancer, studying under Alvin Ailey. As a sideline, she founded a small dance company while working at a full-time job. Her dream was to quit her job and to become the full-time executive director of her dance company. We moved it from a dream to a real possibility by attaching a due date. Carol said she wanted a fast result, but even she gulped when we agreed she would make the move within thirty days.

She had many beliefs and fears that were stopping her from achieving her dream. Carol and I worked intensely through a long session to get clear about her dream and to remove the self-imposed limits that prevented her from reaching it. As we grappled with these issues, she began to "speak her dream," expressing possibility about making it happen, and becoming committed to letting the Magic show up in her life.

*Live your dream by
making deliberate choices,
not just responding
to whatever
life throws your way.*

Carol was surprised and delighted to find that going through the process made her see the dream as bigger than her current reality; this change of perception made her more committed to having the dream than to remaining in the status quo.

One of Carol's concerns had been how she would finance her new venture and support herself at the same time. We designed a plan that enabled her to resign her full-time position and still pay her bills. One of the strategies we used was identifying one of her skills—grant proposal writing—that Carol could use as a free-lancer. Once she realized she didn't need to be a salaried employee, she turned her current employer into her client, and she generated $25,000 of income for herself within the first few months after she was on her own.

Once Carol knew how she would pay the rent, she turned her attention to her new venture. She assembled a board, scheduled recitals, and got into action living her dream. The first major performance of Carol's dance company, which I'm pleased to say I attended, was offered to an audience of more than two hundred people.

REAL PEOPLE: GEORGE

At one time, George had been severely overweight. Through great effort and perseverance, he had trimmed down, and he

COMMIT TO YOUR DREAM.

was feeling great about being thin. Now his dream was to be physically fit, but he was having trouble getting himself motivated to go to the gym three times a week.

In exploring George's life, we discovered that his passion was to live life as an adventure. To George, that meant trying new things, seeking new challenges—in short, George hated feeling bored.

Out of his enthusiasm for testing himself in new situations, George designed a project that would allow him to fulfill his dream adventurously. The project he took on was to train for a triathlon. The venture had George feeling turned on, lit up, passionate, and he had no difficulty getting to the gym with regularity. He even hired a coach to help him break through any limitations.

The more George pushed himself beyond where he was, the more passionate he became. This was inherent in his Purpose, to live life as an adventure. You can ignite your dreams by knowing what you are passionate about.

REAL PEOPLE: THE CARTERS

The Carters are a married couple who owned a computer store in a fancy shopping center. Like many people, their dream was to have financial freedom while having the time to enjoy each other.

After our session, the Carters realized that maintaining their current business was actually working against achieving their dream. The massive overhead in their upscale setting was eroding their profits, and the retail nature of their establishment meant that they were always "on call" when the store was open. They needed more flexibility, and they recognized that to get it, they would have to close the store and change to a new business. They considered this a daring and scary move.

One of the best aspects of the techniques used in this book is

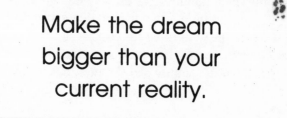

Make the dream bigger than your current reality.

that they can be used to create balance; after all, part of having it all is having the time to enjoy it. The Carters didn't know at first that their dream included closing down their store; it only became clear during the process. They were passionate both about being in business and about having time for each other, but their passion did not include owning a retail operation. Once they were committed to realizing their passion, they were ready to get into action toward having their dream. You will see as their story continues later in this book that they did it in record time.

Allow yourself to get lit up, turned on, and really passionate about your dream.

THE PASSION PYRAMID

Passion is the access to power.
—Marcia Wieder

My techniques for making your dreams come true have several advantages over other approaches. One of the benefits is that you don't have to choose having your dream in one area of your life over getting what you want in others.

I often hear people lament that they could have what they want if they gave up other things, or that they must work endless, tedious hours to earn the kind of money they need. I don't believe it's necessary to make sacrifices like these to have your dream. That is, it's not necessary to forfeit anything you want, providing you are clear about your dream.

When you are passionate, you are focused, intentional, and determined. Your body, mind, and heart are all moving toward the same goal in unison. Richard Bach, in his book *The Bridge Across Forever*, tells us that "passionately obsessed by anything we love—sailboats, airplanes, ideas—an avalanche of magic flattens the way ahead, levels rules, reasons, deserts, bears us with it over chasms, fears, doubts."

Passionate thinking is a driving ambition. It comes from a place within you that provides emotional reinforcement. This energy is what you want to harness in propelling your dreams into reality, and I designed the Passion Pyramid to help you do it.

It is possible to bring passion to whatever you are doing. You can have passion about your current job or project. It is not always necessary to leave where you are in order to have passion. Imagine how different your life might be if you could easily bring passion into your career, your relationships, and even feel passion every day.

The Passion Pyramid is a tool. It will help you see how to get from where you are to where you want to be, while keeping you balanced in all the areas of your life. As you strive to make your dreams come true, the information you put into the Pyramid is the foundation on which everything else rests.

You will find a copy of the Pyramid below. Use it to align the

THE PASSION PYRAMID

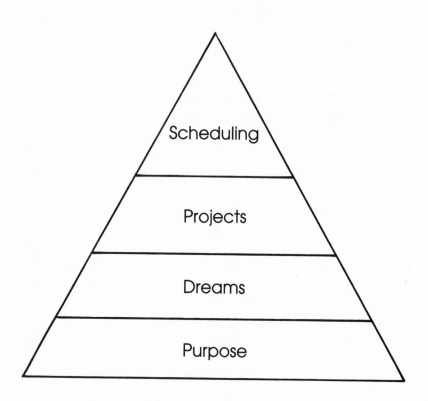

"four Ps" that can ignite your dreams—purpose, passion, possibilities, and power. When used properly, the Pyramid can help you design a blueprint for achieving what you want, and for streamlining the process of reaching your dreams. Like any stable structure, the Pyramid is intended to be used from the bottom up.

Most of us live our lives from the top down. Then something happens—a "fire" that needs to be put out, or something to which you must attend. You look at your calendar (scheduling) to see when you can fit it in. Sometimes, if you're lucky, the activity may be related to a project you're working on or one you intend to start. If you're *very* lucky, the venture may even filter down into one of your dreams.

However, when you start working from the top down, whatever you're doing does not come from your Purpose. You want to get to the top eventually, because that's where the power comes from; but to live a life you love that's filled with passion, you need to start with Purpose and build up from the base. Let's look at how the sections of the Pyramid show up in the world.

Purpose. Your Purpose is the foundation; it answers the question "Who am I?" Some people think they've known the an-

> *Once you know your Purpose, you will be able to create projects that take your dreams out of your imagination and into your reality.*

swer to that question for years. Then, like the captain in the Real People story at the end of this chapter, they are surprised to discover a "different" truth. Later, we'll go through an exercise to help you answer the question "Who am I?"

Dreams. Once you have established your foundation and you know who you are, you can start to look at how you want your life to be. For example, if your Purpose, like George's, is to live life as an adventure, your dreams might include bringing adventure into everything you do, or into a specific aspect of your life like your business or your marriage. All of these are expressions of George's Purpose, "To live life as an adventure." Larry's Purpose, to live life in partnership, helped him to understand his dreams for a close marriage and for powerful partnerships that generate profit. With clarity of Purpose, your dreams develop a deeper meaning and are more likely to manifest.

Projects. Standing in your Purpose, you will be able to develop projects that will take your dreams out of your imagination and make them part of your reality. Not only will your projects be "real," but they will further the journey toward your dream by having built-in, specific, measurable results. Your projects will help you to pro-ject yourself into your future.

PASSION
PERMEATES
EVERYTHING.

Scheduling. Scheduling, at the top of the Pyramid, actually puts your projects onto the calendar, giving you dates by which to meet your objectives and make your dreams come true. The good news is that most of your time, at this point, is spent doing things you love, not just more busywork.

Having assembled the Pyramid, there are three supporting elements that come into play—possibilities, power, and passion.

PASSION PYRAMID

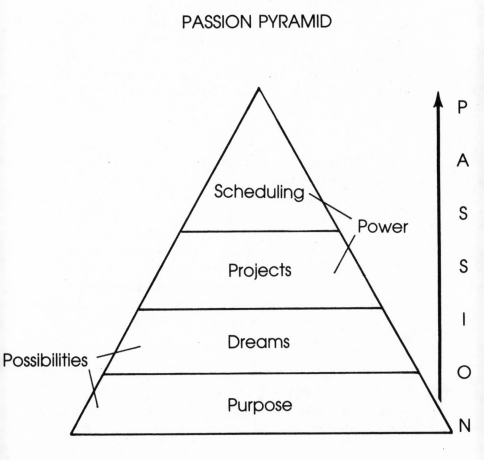

Possibilities. The Purpose and Dreams phases of the Pyramid are filled with possibilities. This is where you dream, imagine, or visualize what you want. It's the "anything goes" section. Looking at the possibilities in your life from the vantage point of your Purpose, you will feel a new level of power and energy. You will see opportunities where you never saw them before, you will have new perspectives about what you can make happen in your life, and you will allow yourself to remain open to the Magic. You'll understand more about this concept as we begin to work with it.

Power. Once your dreams turn into the projects and we add "due dates," you move into a powerful place. We could say it's no longer "just a dream." The power to live your dreams every day results from your ability to be "in action" on your dreams and to measure the specific results of your projects.

Passion. Standing figuratively and emotionally in your Purpose, you will realize that passion permeates everything else. Your Purpose is what excites you, and kindles the passion to make your dreams come true. Remember, passion is the access to power and passion comes from purpose, knowing who you are and what "turns you on."

Notice how the sections of the Pyramid interconnect. For example, passion lives in all areas of your life, but it takes on special meaning as you bring it into your dreams; possibilities can be seen from every vantage point on the Pyramid, but they start to show up in ways you can recognize when you move from dreams to projects. The process is not linear; it is holographic and multidimensional. When you are living a passionate life, it shows up everywhere.

Marcia's Passion Pyramid

I describe my own Purpose in life as "joyously self-expressing." How do I know? Here are some hints: I often wear highly expressive clothes and do outrageous things. One of the highlights

> You can live the
> life that you love
> that is filled
> with passion.

of my life was to win my eighth-grade speech contest. I spoke about being the first woman astronaut and how I would redesign the uniforms and spaceship interior design. Once you meet me, you see instantly that "joyously self-expressing" is who I am, and it's not just my clothes, but actually an attitude, a way of being.

I believe in putting everything I want into my dreams. One dream that represents my Purpose is to travel the world in style and elegance, speaking publicly about something that will make a positive impact on people. I decided to travel on a luxurious cruise ship as a guest speaker, offering workshops about making dreams come true. My project, one of any number I could have created, was a clear expression of my Purpose—to joyously self-express—and an obvious representation of my dream. Once I took my "passion pulse" by checking in to see how excited I was about the idea, I knew that the project was completely consistent with my Purpose.

With specific, measurable results of the project defined, it was easy to get into action. As I gained clarity about what I wanted and created a project to achieve it, the Magic started to show up. The Magic for me was how easily and effortlessly my dream came true. Yes, I did the three strategies that I identified would get this in action, but before I got to item number four, which

PASSION IS THE ACCESS TO POWER.

was "Do phone follow-up on the package I sent," the cruise company called and booked me. At the time, it almost seemed too easy. I spent the Christmas holidays cruising the Hawaiian Islands, all expenses paid.

Don't sabotage yourself by trying to deal with the Pyramid from the top down. For example, most people have a negative reaction to Scheduling, because they feel anxious about finding time to take on additional tasks. Starting at the top of the Pyramid rarely, if ever, allows you to build a life you can live on purpose. Rest assured, however, you will accomplish things faster and easier when you are passionate and on purpose. You will even have more time to do the things you really want to do.

When I first started doing this work some years ago, I used to say, "Every day I'm doing something that I love." Now I can say, "I'm *always* doing things that I love." My office is devoid of files, except for project files. Since the projects come from my dreams, which come, in turn, from my Purpose, I am living a life that I love, one that is filled with passion. Whenever I have extra time, which I often do, I reach for one of my project files. I love working on them because I know that doing so puts me constantly in action on the life I intentionally created for myself.

REAL STORIES: THE CAPTAIN

The "captain" had achieved what he thought was his life's dream. From the time he was seven years old, he had dreamed of being a ship's captain. He held on to the dream for such a long time that when he actually achieved it, he wondered, "Is that all there is?" Passion was missing for him. He wasn't turned on by becoming captain; it was something he'd always thought he would do. After all, his father had been a captain, too.

What had initially been an empowering dream for the captain had become empty over the years. Now, at age forty-five, he found himself longing for the next twenty years to pass, so he could retire at sixty-five and move on to something else. He was appalled: what a terrible waste it would be to wait twenty years to be happy. Then he started to appreciate that there was a different way to live his life, that he could create a new dream that would allow him to remain a sea captain but bring passion into his life every day. He realized he had a talent for finding solutions to difficult problems, even dilemmas that others thought were impossible to resolve. He began to list his skills and, as he did so, he became aware that he was turned on by some of them. He asked me to help him, and we began to turn his passion into projects.

When I last saw the captain, he was beginning to have conversations with engineering and trading companies, exploring

---

Access your passion through your Life's Purpose.

---

the possibilities of working with them when he wasn't at sea. The best news was that he was excited about potential new opportunities, and enthusiastic about some of the new unpredictability of his life. He laughed when he told me he had forgotten how much he liked surprises. He had allowed himself to fall into a rut and, until we got him moving toward his dream, he couldn't see how to get out.

Getting in touch with your passion will always get you out of your rut and onto a higher road. We'll discuss further how this can be done in chapter 10, Projects That Move You Forward.

> *Getting in touch with your passion will always get you out of your rut and onto a higher road.*

REMEMBERING YOUR PURPOSE

The purpose of life is to live a life of purpose.
—*Robert Byrne*

If passion is the access to power, the way to access passion is through your Life's Purpose. Your Purpose is who you are, what gets you excited; I might even say that your Purpose is remembering why you're here. The story about co-creating on the next pages will explain what I mean.

A client once told me, "I made money and I was successful, but I still felt there must be something else."

"Yes, there's something else," I said. "It's called passion, and it comes from living your life on purpose."

If you're like a lot of readers, you might say, "I picked up this book because I wanted to make my dreams come true, but, between you and me, I don't think I have a Purpose."

Yes, you do. Your Purpose is not a big, burdensome, heavy weight that you "must" accomplish in your life; rather, it's an expression of who you are. Larry, who didn't think finding his Purpose was the way to double his business, didn't increase sales until he defined who he was; then it was easy.

A STORY OF CO-CREATING

One day before you were born, while you were still up in heaven, God called you in and said, "It's time for you to go down to earth."

> *Your Purpose is*
> *who you are and*
> *what gets you excited.*
> *Your Purpose is*
> *remembering*
> *why you're here.*

"Oh, do I have to?" you asked. "Do you have a reason or a mission that you want me to accomplish while I'm there?"

"Yes, I do. Your mission is to have everything you desire during your earthly life. Have a seat, and let's co-create the Divine Design of your life."

You and God spoke for a long time, and God elicited every desire you thought would guarantee a fulfilling earthly life. Perhaps you told God you wanted to be a communicator, or a creative artist. Maybe you said that you also wanted a loving family and lots of time to enjoy your life. Maybe you said you just wanted to play.

Once you outlined everything you wanted and actually started looking forward to the adventure, with a snap of the fingers, God dropped you down into the womb of your mother. As you floated around in what felt like a water bed, being nourished within the warm liquid, you started developing amnesia about your conversation with God. One day the lights flashed, you struggled through the birth canal, and made your appearance into the world.

You arrived into a brightly lit room where your lifeline was cut and they spanked your bottom. You were confused; it all happened so fast you forgot what your life was about. You felt that something was wrong—this was not the way it was supposed to be, but you couldn't remember exactly what "it" was.

You can spend a long time trying to remember.

Some people do remember and are living their lives with purpose. History has recorded some of them as the most mission-oriented individuals in the world—Gandhi, Mother Theresa, Martin Luther King. At some point they remembered.

And everyday people like you and me have also remembered what our lives are about.

Remembrance can occur when you're young or old. Many people never remember, and some don't even know that they don't know. Occasionally, people experience a frightening event, such as a heart attack, which causes them to wake up and remember.

Of course, it's not necessary to wait for a life-threatening situation to push you into remembrance. You can just stop what you're doing and say, "Wait a minute, this is not what my life is about." In that moment, with that realization, you start to remember.

Wake up. It's time to remember and start living your life on purpose.

Your Purpose could be anything that gets your juices flowing; it comes from what turns you on in life. The more broadly you state it, the better, because the broader your Purpose, the more room there is for passion and possibility. If you're concerned that your Purpose is not going to be "worthy," or big enough, or decent enough, here are some examples that others have offered when asked to complete the sentence "My life's Purpose is . . .":

   . . . to live life as an adventure.

   . . . to create joy.

. . . to teach or learn.

. . . to be available when people need me.

. . . to make a difference.

. . . to go beyond.

. . . to play and have fun.

Your Purpose is anything that touches your heart and makes a difference to you. If you're working at a job just for the money, and what you're doing doesn't make you feel proud, perhaps you've lost your sense of Purpose. The test is how you feel: are you turned on, or do you rationalize by saying that if you don't "sell this product, somebody else will," or "If I don't stay here, where will I go? What will I do? How will I pay my bills?"

Most people are so busy reacting to the needs of daily life that they're happy just to be getting through the day. It's hard to live on Purpose when life revolves around daily crises and you're always feeling overwhelmed. By taking the time to define your Purpose, you'll open up more time and space, have more energy, and be more focused.

Defining Your Purpose

You may be wondering how to determine your Purpose. Don't worry, you don't have to do it all at once, and certainly not permanently and for all time. Life flows and ebbs, and your Purpose may modify accordingly over time.

When I first started speaking about my own Purpose, I didn't describe it as "to joyously self-express." I began by looking at what I enjoyed doing, decided that I like to talk and travel, so I defined my Life's Purpose as "Talking and Traveling." I saw that traveling was part of a dream, answering the question of how I want my life to be, rather than a purpose, describing who I am. Over time, that description was honed and sharpened, and yours will be, too; the more you work with it, the more it will start to resonate as a unique definition of who you are. Eventually, you will create a way to speak about it that really describes it for you. This is important. The more easily you can speak about or think about your Purpose, the more accessible it will be to you. You want it to be instantly accessible, like your name.

The five-minute exercise on page 32 will help you begin to get in touch with your Life's Purpose by looking at your past accomplishments or special moments. One place to look for what turns you on is to see what has turned you on in the past. Don't think that your life is devoid of passion; everyone has special moments. As a matter of fact, if this exercise is hard, begin by examining the way in which you perceive yourself.

Accomplishments can be as simple as having been graduated from college, meeting a spouse, getting a big raise. If you can't find at least three accomplishments—and I promise you've had at least thirty-three, maybe three hundred and thirty-three— you're being too hard on yourself and setting your sights too high.

It doesn't even matter if you harbor negative reactions about your accomplishments. When you look back now, were you excited? Did you feel good or proud? If you answer "Yes" to those questions, write it down.

When the exercise is completed, take a deep breath and relax; the hard part is over. Now look for the pattern (and it's important to look broadly). Look for the common component that made you feel good about those achievements. What was present for you in all three examples? What were you passionate about?

If you think at first that there's nothing consistent about the listed deeds, bring your mind back to the time and place of each situation. Get in touch with what you were feeling then, about the events and about yourself. Avoid narrowing things down; try to stay with broad, generic statements. Perhaps all the items listed were fun; they all had a partnership component; or they all made you feel uneasy at first, but you did them anyway.

The commonality need not be that all the events happened in the same season of the year; what you're looking for is the consistency of how you felt in each case—who you were being —not what was happening externally. Perhaps the accomplish-

GETTING IN TOUCH WITH YOUR LIFE'S PURPOSE

List below three times in your life from the day you were born to this moment when you accomplished something about which you were proud or passionate. Look for three successes about which you can say, ``I did that; it felt good.'' It could be something you did on your own or with others, or something you did for someone else. Perhaps it was having your first child, buying your first house, a speech you gave in high school or college, a project at work. Write them down simply and quickly; as you write the first one, the other two will come.

1. _____

_____

_____

2. _____

_____

_____

3. _____

_____

_____

ments all went beyond what you thought was possible, or they led to other things that you hadn't even considered. Maybe there was a quality of Magic connected to them, or they were things you made happen against all odds. The broader the common thread is, the better.

The acid test is whether or not the consistent element was something about which you felt excited; however, don't be concerned if passion seems to elude you at first. Some people feel passion about their Purpose as soon as they define it. Others may not be sure if the stated Purpose is something that truly excites them. You may not experience passion until you're in action on a project; someone else may be turned on by the planning process. If you're having difficulty finding the common thread in all three accomplishments, but you were excited by two of them, you're probably on the right track.

Speaking Your Purpose

Using language that incorporates your newly defined Purpose into your speech will affirm your passion and move you toward having your dream. I call this "speaking your Purpose," and below I've listed some examples from people with whom I've

> Your purpose in life
> is simply to help
> the purpose of
> the Universe.
> —George Bernard Shaw

worked. In each case, the three accomplishments are listed, followed by the first try at identifying their Life's Purpose and then their second attempt to speak it in an empowering way. Note that the initial descriptions of Purpose were altered later into a short and memorable "soundbite" that could easily be retained and recalled.

Accomplishments	Purpose
1. Receiving his certified public accountant's certificate.	To add value to everything he does.
2. Being promoted to manager at work.	Or
3. Buying a dream house while selling his old home without a broker.	To make a difference by being different.
1. Growing her business.	To use her creativity to alter other people's lives.
2. Having a special relationship with a great person.	Or
3. Rearing two fabulous children	To inspire people into action.
1. Making it to the U.S. National Racquetball Team.	To have fun while being the best that she can be.
2. Becoming racquetball state champion.	Or
3. Striving for a professional career in racquetball.	To go for the gold.
1. Having twin daughters.	To experience the adventure of people and life.
2. Experiences in the wilderness.	Or
3. Winning the Small Business Administration's Outstanding Businesswoman Award.	To live life as an adventure.

SPEAKING PASSIONATELY
ABOUT YOUR PURPOSE

Using the lines below, list all the different ways in which you can complete the following sentence so that, when you think about it and when you speak about it, you feel its underlying passion. Use your three accomplishments to help you.

My Life's Purpose is:

_____

_____

_____

_____

_____

_____

Now rephrase your Purpose to speak it in an empowering way. Create a "soundbite." Keep it short and simple.

_____

_____

_____

_____

_____

_____

It doesn't matter whether your Purpose is single-focused or multidimensional. Imagine using the zoom lens of a camera to capture your Life's Purpose in the most general way. Then play with the picture until the form, sound, and "feel" of it are right for you. The writing exercise on page 35 will help you find validating and empowering words to access the passion in your Purpose.

The next step is to enter your Purpose in the appropriate section at the base of the Passion Pyramid. When your Purpose

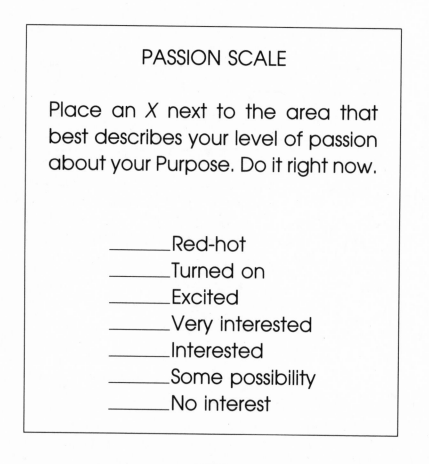

PASSION SCALE

Place an *X* next to the area that best describes your level of passion about your Purpose. Do it right now.

_____Red-hot

_____Turned on

_____Excited

_____Very interested

_____Interested

_____Some possibility

_____No interest

has been entered in the designated block, describe it in some detail and in a way that makes you feel its passion. You will find the Passion Pyramid repeated throughout the book, so you can fill in additional categories as you make choices that will allow your dreams to become reality. You will also find the Passion Scale, appearing for the first time on page 36, duplicated several times in these pages, so that you can rate your passion or take your passion pulse as we move through each stage. Rate how you feel about your Life's Purpose. If you are at "interested" or below, see what's missing from your Purpose that would "turn you on" and add it. If your past experiences have only provided an "interesting" life, maybe make the decision here and now to consciously design in the noun, verb, or adjective that will add more passion to your Purpose, and ultimately to your life.

Then rate your passion again.

DREAMS: HOW DO YOU WANT YOUR LIFE TO BE?

*Go confidently in the direction of your
dreams. Live the life you have imagined.*
—Henry David Thoreau

Now that you've discovered the passion underlying your Purpose, the focus will be on the direction in which your life will be moving. You'll need some additional tools on the journey to make your dreams come true; in this chapter, you'll learn how to formulate dreams that will steer you on the right course.

Perhaps you're wondering about the difference between your Purpose and your dreams. Your Purpose is fundamental: it's who you are. Dreams are mechanisms by which to bring your Purpose, deliberately, into day-to-day life.

Dreams answer the question "How do you want your life to be?"

Dreams also can help eliminate those aspects of life that are inconsistent with your Purpose. For example, my own Purpose is to joyously self-express; some dreams may make me happy, while others may not allow any Magic into my life. By measuring my dreams against my Purpose, I can tell if what I've chosen will move me forward with passion to live the life I want, or is more about a "should," a duty or a self-imposed responsibility.

This activity is not intended to turn obligations into dreams. Yes, you have to pay the rent and handle other responsibilities, but those activities get scheduled into reality anyway.

Creating dreams is about getting your life where you want it to be. For instance, if you have a specific financial issue, create a financial dream within the area that expresses who you are. The financial dream for a person who wants to live life as an adventure may be different from the financial dream for someone who wants to be in a committed family relationship.

Developing dreams is part of the process for gaining insight into what matters or doesn't matter to you. This is different from the traditional goal-setting process in business, where a desired outcome is selected and a completion date is designated. Here, we're after eliminating inconsistencies; these dreams are to be fulfilled in support of your Life's Purpose.

To achieve your dream, everything from this point forward needs to be done from the perspective of your Purpose. Keep checking in, making sure you're passionate about your dreams.

I call this "standing in your Life's Purpose," meaning that it's essential to "be" the Purpose you defined at the foundation of the Passion Pyramid. Even though you may not feel at ease yet with the stated Purpose, assume that you do; the comfort from living life on purpose will follow. Just trust.

It's too early in the process to expect that everything in your life will be in alignment with your Purpose. In fact, while you're learning this process of living from your purpose, it may make more sense to focus on one particular facet of your life. To help you choose which aspects you want to concentrate on, use the Dream Areas exercise on pages 42–43. Decide not only which

Perhaps you hear a small voice saying that you can't have what you want, that you don't have the time or the resources to take on anything else. Don't worry about those nagging sounds; you don't have to ``do'' anything yet. Neither do you have to base new dreams on the past.

Right now, you simply have to ``be'' who you say you are; you can create a whole new life from this moment forward. Ask yourself what dreams a person with your Life's Purpose would want.

Then, listen for the answers.

areas you want to pinpoint, but what there is about them that needs attention.

Perhaps your relationships are boring, and you want to establish relationships that are fun. Maybe you want to become involved in your community in a more creative, innovative, or substantive way than before. Use the Dream Areas form to list the facets of your life and what there is to explore about them; there is a visualization exercise later in this chapter to guide you through the actual exploration.

When the Dream Areas form has been completed, review it and choose one category to use as a model for going through this book. When you've mastered one area by following it through to the book's conclusion, you can go back and use the same techniques to make your dreams come true in the other areas of your life. Once you see that this works and how easy it is, you'll be more motivated to apply it to all areas.

Remember that your dreams are both the way to incorporate your Purpose into daily life and a tool for eliminating inconsistencies. Be sure that there is no disparity between the dreams listed on the Dream Areas form and your Life's Purpose. One way to do that is to role-play—to ''be'' your Life's Purpose—and to ask, ''If this is who I am as my Life's Purpose, is this an appropriate dream? Does it line up? Does it turn me on?''

Don't carry any dreams over from an ''old list'' or from what your parents wanted; the values you develop now are the ones by which to live your future life. If you develop dreams that seem contradictory, don't worry that you can't figure out right now how you're going to ''have it all.'' We will get to the ''how'' section in chapter 11.

Suppose you want both a stable home life and exciting world travel. Believe it's possible to take your stable home life on the road, or that you'll discover a whole new set of possibilities to enable you to have them both. You aren't looking for inconsistencies among your dreams, but for dreams that are incompatible with your Purpose. When you respond to the question ''Is this an appropriate dream for my Purpose?,'' you want to feel excited about the answer. Use the Passion Scale to check in and see how you feel about each dream area.

Eventually, you will want Magic to appear in every facet of

DREAM AREAS TO EXPLORE

The categories listed below are aspects of life you might want to explore initially. You don't have to limit yourself to these; select areas that are important to you.

If my Life's Purpose is _____

_____

My Community dream is _____

_____

My Family dream is _____

_____

My Financial dream is _____

_____

My Fitness dream is _____

_____

My Friendship dream is _____

_____

My Fun dream is _____

_____

My Health/Well-being dream is _____

_____

My Outrageous dream is _____

_____

My Personal dream is _____

_____

My Professional dream is_____

_____

My Recreational dream is_____

_____

My Relationships dream is_____

_____

My other dreams are_____

_____

PASSION SCALE

Place an *X* next to the area that best describes your level of passion about your dreams. If you were living the dreams you just wrote, how do you think you would feel? Do it right now.

_____Red-hot
_____Turned on
_____Excited
_____Very interested
_____Interested
_____Some possibility
_____No interest

your life. For the moment, focus on the area you chose to explore throughout this book. The Magic Carpet Ride, a meditation exercise found on page 44, will help you to appraise the dreams in your life, and to align them with your Purpose.

Let's walk through my own example of the Magic Carpet process that I used to focus on the professional area of my life.

When I climbed onto the Magic Carpet, I felt completely at ease, because it was made of my Purpose—to joyously self-express. Fueled by possibility, the Magic Carpet allowed exploration of my professional dream: to have a new career that expresses who I am in the world.

Filled with the passion coming from my Purpose, I created the professional dream to have work that's a joyous expression of who I am. That means having work that is play, that is lucrative, and that allows plenty of time for family, friends, and travel.

THE MAGIC CARPET RIDE

This is a visualization exercise to help you create dreams that are consistent with your Life's Purpose. You may want to read this page into a tape recorder, then play it back. The key to the Magic Carpet is passion. The passion lives inside your heart and is always present when you're living on purpose. Begin by closing your eyes . . . take several deep breaths. Relax.

With your eyes closed, envision a beautiful carpet in front of you. It's exactly the right size for you, and it's decorated with your favorite patterns and colors. It looks so inviting that you're drawn to it; the Magic Carpet is your Purpose.

Go to the Magic Carpet and sit or lie comfortably on it. Relax; you feel completely ``at home'' living on purpose.

The Magic Carpet's fuel is possibility, the knowledge that what you want can become your reality. Powered by possibility, the Magic Carpet starts to lift off the ground, gently and slowly, and you suddenly find yourself outdoors, floating through a fragrant breeze.

It's a beautiful day; the sky is clear blue with puffy white clouds, and the air is the right temperature. You're completely relaxed and at ease in your Purpose, filled with passion, knowing there's unlimited possibility everywhere.

As you look around, you see that the Magic Carpet is being

drawn into a clearing. This is your destination, a place that is gently pulling you toward it by its power. The Magic Carpet slows, and, easily and gently, it sets down.

You reinforce your sense of Purpose by finishing the sentence ''My Life's Purpose is . . .'' You feel grounded in your Purpose, and from that perspective, you begin to look at how you want life to be.

Keeping your eyes closed, look at the area of your life you chose to explore. If you are focusing on the professional area, from the perspective of your Purpose complete the sentence ''My dream in the professional area is to . . .'' Perhaps you'd like to open your eyes and write it down; if you prefer to keep your eyes closed, fill it in at the end.

After you've finished exploring the area you selected, relax in perfect comfort on the Magic Carpet. Take a last look around and experience the power that envelops you. Feel the clarity of your Life's Purpose, and know that your dream in the area you examined is in perfect alignment with your Purpose.

When you've completed the Magic Carpet Ride, you will have identified at least one dream in your chosen area. You can have more than one if you wish, but it's less important to designate many dreams than it is to be clear that the dreams express your Life's Purpose.

When you're ready to leave the Magic Carpet, breathe deeply. Relax. Open your eyes at your own pace. You will have a clear memory of everything that happened during the Magic Carpet Ride. Write it down on the Passion Pyramid: ''My Life's Purpose is . . . ,'' and, in the area you chose, ''My dream is to . . .''

Although the Magic Carpet Ride focused on my professional life, that's not the only area for which I have developed dreams. In the personal area, my dream is to develop partnerships with individuals who are creative visionaries so we can produce results that have a positive impact on others. In the area of well-being, it's to be healthier and more physically fit at forty than I was at thirty. In the area of relationships, it's to be in a loving partnership with my life's companion. In the area of friendship, it's to have friends worldwide. In the financial area, it's to shop without looking at price tags. Notice that each dream is an expression of my purpose.

Don't be stingy when you develop dreams; put into them everything that you want. When I noted that one of my dreams

THE PASSION PYRAMID

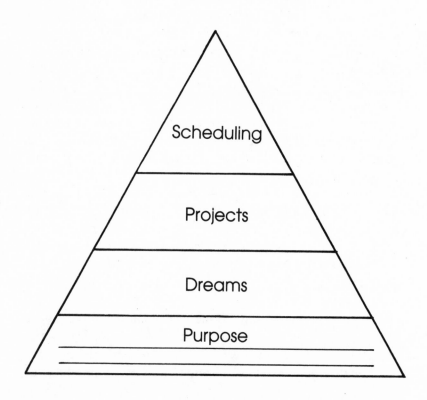

Scheduling

Projects

Dreams

Purpose

is to have friends worldwide, I didn't say merely that I wanted friends. I am committed to having friends everywhere on the planet, which suggests travel as another dream. If you don't develop your objectives in a way that expresses your Life's Purpose, your ability to make your dreams come true will be short-circuited.

The power that you experience all around you on the Magic Carpet Ride comes from having passion within you. However, you don't have to be doing this exercise to feel the excitement.

In the designated space on page 48, commit yourself to focusing on one specific area of your life by filling in the blank. Then, on page 46, write your Purpose once again in the foundation of the Passion Pyramid and write the dream you'll be working on. This dream will allow you to walk through the entire Making Your Dreams Come True process. Then you can use this process on all the other dream areas. For example, my own Life's Pur-

When you're standing in your Life's Purpose, the passion is always there and possibilities live everywhere.

You feel powerful, and capable of making your dreams come true.

pose is to joyously self-express, and my dream in the professional area is to have work that expresses who I am in the world. Fill in your Purpose and dream.

When you fill in the base of the Pyramid, commit your Purpose to paper fully and with passion, and describe the dream by which you will live your life on purpose.

Fill in the blank by writing in the aspect of your life on which you intend to concentrate.

I am committed to focusing on a specific area of my life at this time. The area that I'm going to focus on is_____

A DREAM THAT INSPIRES YOU

All our dreams can come true if we
have the courage to pursue them.
—Walt Disney

A dear friend once told me that turning dreams into projects is a way to pro-ject yourself into the future. In this chapter, you will learn how to define your dream, how to develop it, and how to initiate it in the form of a project.

Clarifying the dream is the critical component that most people omit, largely because the dream isn't perceived as something real, specific, and attainable. If your dream comes from your Purpose, a project can be created to make your dream a reality.

The power to develop a viable project depends, first, on your ability to define your dream in a way that inspires you. The project, which will have specific, measurable results, makes the dream attainable. Moreover, Magic will appear as new possibilities open up during the definition phase, and you can start to launch yourself into a different dimension of living life.

Sometimes defining a dream is as simple as choosing a date by which it will happen. Other times, the definition is not as simple as it sounds—having a general idea of how you want your dream to be may not be enough to know exactly how to achieve it.

Describing Your Dream to a "T"
When a dream first enters consciousness, you may not be able to see with clarity what it looks like. Often a dream starts in the

---

Dreams are
a way to
PRO-JECT yourself
into the future.

---

subconscious, and remains a nebulous idea floating around in the back of the mind. In order for your dream to come true, it is essential to get it "out of your head."

There are many different ways to gain access to the details of your dream. Some people like to do it through a writing exercise; some carry on conversations with others about their dream; and some prefer talking into a tape recorder. One client told me she actually thinks by talking.

I have provided room on pages 51 and 52 for you to write out all the aspects of your dream. Use the worksheet to help you get started. This exercise is a powerful way to get the dream out of your head and allow it to begin living as part of reality. Use this to get in touch with all the resources that can help to develop your dream; use it also to get a clear image of what you want, to get the level of detail behind the initial statement of your dream. Then use the Details of My Dream page (page 53) to bring it all together in narrative form. Notice whether you believe it's possible to have your dream, but don't let your beliefs limit you. We'll deal with your beliefs shortly.

If you aren't happy with what you write down at first, you aren't committed to leaving it there. Rewrite it, more than once if necessary. As you start to gain clarity, what gets committed to paper will begin to feel right. At the end of this chapter, there are

MY DREAM, ASSUMING
UNLIMITED RESOURCES—WORKSHEET

Describe your dream. _____
_____
_____

What are you doing? _____
_____
_____

Where are you doing it? _____
_____
_____

How do you feel? _____
_____
_____

How do you look? _____
_____
_____

Who are you with? _____
_____
_____

What does your day look like? _____
_____
_____

What are you creating or accomplishing?_____

_____

_____

Give some detail._____

_____

_____

Give more detail._____

_____

_____

some Real People stories that will illustrate how these techniques work for people who have passion in their Purpose and define their dreams accordingly.

Seeking Inspiration

The specifics of your dream may not all come at one sitting; perhaps it will take a few days, even a few weeks. You may need to seek inspiration to complete the exercise: go to the library, to plays or movies; rent children's videos like *Beauty and the Beast* and *Mary Poppins*; you might want to travel.

Another great place to find out about your waking dream is from the dreams you have while sleeping. No doubt you've heard this recommendation before, but it's worth repeating: place a pad or a cassette recorder next to your bed. Tell yourself before you fall asleep to remember your nocturnal dreams, and eventually you will. In fact, you can plant a question in your subconscious before going to sleep—"I want more information about my waking dream"—and see what comes up during the night.

You also can daydream by relaxing and letting your mind

DETAILS OF MY DREAM

Complete the following sentences with as many details of your dream as you can summon. Put your dream into a narrative form and feel free to use pictures or diagrams.

Play with it; use your imagination; try different alternatives. Write down something that you want in your dream, and if it doesn't feel right, change it. You are the author of your own dream.

My dream, in detail, includes:_____

_____

_____

_____

_____

_____

_____

_____

_____

_____

_____

_____

_____

wander. Be alert to what excites you: perhaps you admire some-body's beautiful office, somebody's lovely home, parts of a job someone else is performing. When you are building your dream and delineating its details, feel free to include in your own reality what you like in the reality of other people. This is one place "plagiarizing" really pays off.

> *If there is something simple that can be brought into your life right now that will make you feel good, do it and begin to live your dream immediately.*

Perhaps you're a woman who wants a beautiful dress from a particular designer. Maybe your dream can start with something small, like an accessory or a great pair of new shoes. Make an investment in yourself and bring part of your dream into reality; you will be that much closer to having it all.

Some people clarify their dreams by using photographs. Per-haps you want to live near the ocean and have a view of the mountains. Find a picture of what you want, put it into your reality by posting it on the bathroom mirror, and start connect-ing to it. If you begin to think about it as existing now, it will eventually become real and you will recognize it when it does.

Whatever you do to stimulate your mind, pay attention and notice what feels good. Relax and have a good time. You are creating a design for your life, letting your dream come forward and elaborating on it. Remember, this is your dream; you don't have to choose what you don't want, or what you think you should have, or what you've always had, or what your mother wanted you to have.

Start by thinking about it as real, by visualizing it and expanding on your visualization. Learn to speak about it clearly; the more you speak about it, the more detailed it will become. Write, plan, and brainstorm about it. Get into action, any kind of action. It's your dream; start living it now.

Now, rate yourself on the Passion Scale. How do you feel about the possibility of your dream? How will you feel when this dream comes true?

REAL PEOPLE: GEORGE

George's Purpose, to live life as an adventure, was embodied by his general goal: to bring adventure into every facet of his life. However, George was having trouble finding a way to accomplish his dream, which was to take a lengthy, luxurious fishing trip to a tropical location.

When George first started to speak about his dream, he had so many reasons why he couldn't have it. Initially, it was difficult for him to speak about it, but the more he spoke about it, the more committed he became. Once he learned to stand in his Purpose, the dream stopped living as a fuzzy thing in the back of his mind and started to take on structure. He began to paint a word picture of what the dream would look like. He described how he was going to get from one location to another, and the detailed components of his dream.

George asked himself questions and gave himself answers, putting into writing exactly what his dream would look like,

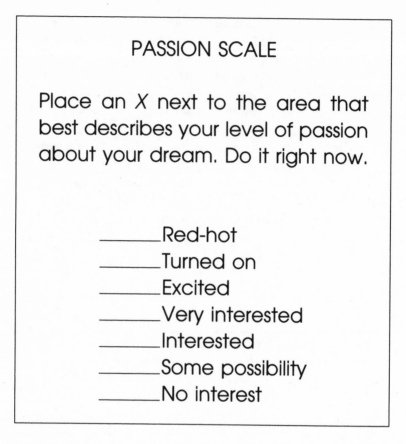

PASSION SCALE

Place an *X* next to the area that best describes your level of passion about your dream. Do it right now.

_____Red-hot

_____Turned on

_____Excited

_____Very interested

_____Interested

_____Some possibility

_____No interest

making it up and having fun doing so. The first question George asked was how long he wanted the dream trip to be. He was surprised to discover that he wanted it to last at least a month. Who else was with him? He was alone. Where was he living? It was a tropical paradise.

As he wrote, George came up with more and more questions, and as he answered them, he became more and more clear about his dream. For instance, he decided to forsake his alarm clock and sleep until he awakened naturally. Even though he was living in a tropical paradise, he still wanted the *Wall Street Journal* delivered daily, because he didn't want to be completely out of touch with the world. He didn't want to do any cooking, so he saw himself jogging on the beach and returning to a delicious breakfast prepared by a chef. Some of these details might seem silly to you, but this was George's dream, and he put in everything he wanted and left out what he didn't want.

Then George started to ask himself more about how he would spend the day. He visualized possessing a small fishing boat; he saw himself using the boat to take fishing trips, both for fun and for the opportunity to meet other people. He kept designing into his dream all that he wanted.

George also expressed some concern about being away for an extended period of time. He wondered what impact his trip would have on the people and the business he was leaving behind. He tempered his anxiety by answering these questions positively: he decided, and his family verified, that they would function well in his absence, and that his business would continue to generate profits.

Once he was clear about his dream, George resolved to try it out on a short-term basis. His new clarity inspired him. He

PICTURE YOURSELF ALREADY LIVING YOUR DREAM.

determined that, within three months, he would take a two-week fishing trip to an exotic place. He chose Costa Rica, he scheduled it, and he went.

George had a wonderful time, and he learned a few important things. The first lesson was that two weeks was long enough. The fishing was great and so was the adventure, but he missed his family, and after two weeks he had had enough of doing the same thing every day.

He also observed that bringing adventure into his life deepened his relationship with his family. There's renewed romance in his marriage, and now, anytime he chooses to do so, he's able to bring adventure into many different areas of his life. George discovered, and you will, too, that one magical adventure can lead to many more, if we stop holding back and go for what we want.

REAL PEOPLE: BRIAN

Brian's Purpose was to make a contribution to society. His professional dream was to integrate his skills and expertise into a career that he loved. His project was to create a new community service foundation.

The problem was that Brian didn't know what his new foun-

The more you speak and write about your dream, the sooner you'll live it.

---

dation would do. He had a general sense of what he wanted, but he was stymied about the particulars.

Brian decided to create a problem-solving organization to design and implement creative social projects for children and their families. Then he set a specific time, selecting the first of the new year as the date by which he would be open for business.

Still, Brian didn't know what his dream looked like. As he worked to flesh out the details, he saw that the foundation would train people to become visionary community leaders and to develop ongoing support networks. He envisioned creating and marketing a variety of products that would further the mission of the new foundation—a children's radio show, a newsletter, periodicals about literacy, a videotape training series.

Brian now felt able to begin identifying the features of the new organization and also to define where it would be located, how his office would be decorated, what the logo would look like, who would staff it, how the foundation would be perceived in the community, and where he would get funding. The clarity of his dream kept him inspired and in action. As he moved forward, his next steps became more obvious and, in turn, he became more motivated than ever. There was no stopping him now.

> *Discovery consists of*
> *seeing what everybody*
> *has seen and thinking*
> *what nobody has thought.*

REAL PEOPLE: LARRY

Larry, whose Purpose was creating powerful partnerships and intimate relationships, had as his dream to become a partner with anyone at any time that he chose. At first, Larry's dream was to double his income—a big dream without any definition. Envisioning the details of what his dream would look like, Larry decided that his department would have earnings of $3 million by the end of the year, and $10 million within five years.

The more Larry wrote about his dream, the more specific he became. He wanted everyone in his company to be working in partnership. He wanted to be well known, and respected as a leader in his field. He wanted the people with whom he worked to have the best credentials and to offer the highest-quality service. Larry chose a date by which he wanted to have at least three domestic offices, although eventually he wanted branches worldwide. He wanted to be the owner of his office building and have his name on the outside of it. He wanted a personal assistant, a right-hand person who would take good care of him.

Finally, Larry understood that it was possible to determine how the whole dream would look, not just the financial aspect that had been his first concern. Gaining clarity about the entire dream, Larry was able to create projects that would help him achieve it.

The bridge to make all dreams
come true is our thoughts
and our words.

WHERE YOU ARE AND WHERE YOU WANT TO BE

We can chart our future clearly and wisely only
when we know the path which led to the present.
—Adlai E. Stevenson

You have begun to gain some clarity about where you want to be in life, but the road to your dreams starts with where you are now. You can't travel that road successfully if you don't know where you are now, or if where you're standing is made of quicksand.

An honest assessment of your current situation may lead to the disappointing discovery that you're not even close to where you intend to go. Your challenge is to use whatever your existing position is, no matter how far it is from the dream, as a tool to create the momentum to move forward.

Where you are now
is simply
where you are now.
There is no
value judgment
attached to it.

I can't stress enough the importance of making an honest assessment of where you are now. Starting with inaccurate information will lead to erroneous decisions about what has to be done, and how far you have to go, to reach your dream. You cannot design your new life on a strong base if you deny any part of your present existence. Get everything out on the table; list where you are with respect to each of the facets. Be brutally honest, but don't become discouraged; everyone has a number of perceived obstacles to having the life they want.

No doubt you will find that you're at a different place within each aspect of your life—closer to your dream in some and farther away from it in others. That's a typical pattern. Ask yourself where you are not only with respect to your dream, but with regard to your support system, your financial aspects, your feelings. What are your concerns and beliefs? We'll look more closely at attitudes in the next chapter; right now, it's important merely to recognize that you have opinions about where you are compared with where you want to be.

If you need a clue about where to start evaluating, take another look at the completed Dream Areas form in chapter 4. For example, where are you currently with respect to the personal, professional, health, and family aspects of your life? What concerns do you have in these areas? Do you worry that going for your dream will take more time than there is available? Perhaps you don't believe it's possible to make your dream come true.

Tension Can Be Your Friend

In his ground-breaking book, *The Path of Least Resistance,* Robert Fritz suggests the following exercise: picture the tension in a rubber band as you pull on it, and the release of tension as you relax the pull. Tension will resolve itself naturally in whatever direction there is more focus. Therefore, all things being equal, something will move in whichever direction it is pulled harder.

Thus, if you put "where you want to be" at the top of the

*The difference between
where you are
and where you want to be
will create healthy tension
that can move you forward.*

rubber band, and place "where you are" at the bottom of
the rubber band, the difference between where you are and
where you want to be will create tension. It's like pulling the
rubber band in two opposite directions; the direction in which
you pull harder is the way the rubber band is going to snap. If
you tug it intensely toward where you want to be, it will snap in
that direction; if you pull it toward where you already are, it will
snap back.

If you know with clarity where you want to go, focus your
attention on your dream, and use the information about where
you are to propel yourself forward. If you're at level one, for
example, and you want to go to level six, staying focused on
level six will propel you with greater force than if you wanted
to get to six from level three. If you get to level three and you
think, "Look how far I've come already, I can relax now,"
you're likely to remain at level three, or even slide back to
level one. If you find that you're far removed from your goal,
don't despair; the tension in the distance from where you are
to where you want to be may launch you even faster in the
direction you chose.

You can't be thrust forward, however, unless you stay clear
and honest about your current position. When you start to nego-

tiate with yourself—"Oh, it's not so bad; I've been at level one for a couple of years, a little while longer won't hurt"—you dilute or eliminate the dynamic. It's the tension that moves you forward.

Conflict Manipulation

There's a different kind of energy involved when moving toward what you want than there is when moving away from what you don't want. For instance, you may have a problem about debt. If you take action just to eradicate the debt, such as save more and spend less, you're likely to stop taking action as the problem starts to go away. Your inaction can then lead right back to the problem.

Consider the example of countries whose people are starving. In the past, the action we've taken is to feed those who are

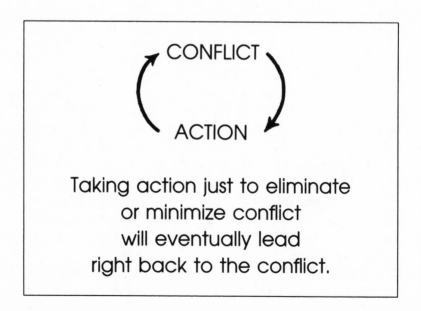

CONFLICT

ACTION

Taking action just to eliminate
or minimize conflict
will eventually lead
right back to the conflict.

hungry. As soon as people are no longer starving, the number of births increases, the population becomes restless, and the problem is increased. In other words, since some progress has been made, people don't try as hard; they feel they can let up a bit in light of what they've already done, and soon they're back to where they started. Manipulating the conflict always leads back to the conflict. One solution is to feed those who are hungry while simultaneously teaching them how to produce food for themselves.

To avoid manipulating the conflict, set up your life so that you're always moving toward what you want. Someone whose dream is to be healthy and physically fit might be fifty pounds overweight in current reality. If the dream is to be healthy and vibrant, to feel and look good, a different kind of energy will be applied than to the drudgery of getting rid of the weight by diet and exercise. In the latter scenario, the food intake tends to increase and the exercise tends to stop as soon as the weight begins to drop.

The critical question becomes whether you're more committed to remaining where you are or to getting where you want to be. The difference between the two is what will propel you forward. On pages 66–67 is an exercise you can use to create a written list of where you are and where you want to be.

As you look at where you are, you are likely to hear an inner voice whispering all your limitations—all your attitudes and beliefs, concerns, fears, worries, and tales about why you can't have what you want.

Fortunately, your positive attitudes and beliefs also will arise —that is, you do believe your dream is possible, it's something you've always wanted, something to which you're committed, something you know you can have.

People frequently sabotage themselves by putting their attitudes, beliefs, or fears into their dream. This is a critical point.

POSITIONING YOURSELF

List where you are in each of the areas of your life compared to where you want to be with respect to your dream. Be brutally honest; you can't know where you want to go until you know with certainty where you are now. Don't judge; just write it all down.

Category	Where I Am Now	Where I Want to Be
Personal	_____	_____
	_____	_____
Professional	_____	_____
	_____	_____
Family	_____	_____
	_____	_____
Friends	_____	_____
	_____	_____
Health/ Well-being	_____	_____
	_____	_____
Financial	_____	_____
	_____	_____

Fun   _____   _____

            _____   _____

Recreation _____   _____

            _____   _____

Relationships _____   _____

            _____   _____

Fitness   _____   _____

            _____   _____

Community   _____   _____

            _____   _____

Other/   _____   _____
Outrageous _____   _____

If you're putting your concerns into your dreams, your fears will become bigger and seem more real as you move closer to getting what you want. Your concerns don't belong in your dream; they're part of where you are now, not where you're going. For example, if your dream is to be successful, write in the Where I Am Now section the fear that you won't have time for friends and family. Assume for the Where I Want to Be section that, in achieving the dream, you will have all the time you desire to enjoy your success, your friends, and your family.

Creating a record of where you are compared to where you want to be is an effective exercise. Write it out and you will have

> # Are you more committed to remaining where you are or to getting where you want to be?

it available to use as positive reinforcement, especially as you move toward your dream.

Reread the exercise whenever you want to ensure that where you want to be is clearly defined, and devoid of your fears about getting there.

BREAKING THROUGH BARRIERS AND BELIEFS

We can achieve what
we can conceive and
believe.
—*Mark Twain*

Everyone has attitudes and beliefs about the aspects of their lives. Your opinions are long-term parts of who you are: if you're thirty years old, they've been developing for thirty years; if you're forty, they've been evolving for forty years. Attitudes and beliefs are not always negative and not always barriers to achieving what you want; even if they are, fear not, it's possible to use them to your advantage.

The decisions and choices you make ultimately result from the attitudes and beliefs you hold about everything in your life. The process looks like this:

Attitudes & Beliefs
< create >
Thoughts & Feelings
< which create >
Choices & Decisions

Attitudes and beliefs are at the core of how you react in the world. No matter how or why you developed them, it's crucial that you take responsibility for them, and that you evaluate them honestly. The naked truth about your attitudes and beliefs in this chapter is as important as your honest assessment in the last chapter of "where you are" versus "where you want to be."

In my workshops I often ask, "How many people believe they can make their dreams come true?" A few hands go up. Then I ask, "How many believe it's *possible* to make your dreams come true?" Most hands go up.

"So what will it take to move you from possible to probable?" I ask. The answer is "believing it." You either believe this or not, and that's your belief about your beliefs. Again, the difference between believing you can change a belief and actually changing a belief is believing it. Do you believe it's that basic? Notice your belief.

Then I inquire, "Who's living in the home of their dreams, driving the car of their dreams, is in the relationship or job of their dreams?" Sadly, few respond favorably.

If you believe it's possible to make your dreams come true, yet you don't do it, there's a gap between where you are and where you want to be. This gap comprises your attitudes and beliefs. The bigger the negative beliefs, the wider the gap.

Some attitudes and beliefs are positive and supportive of the overall dream, and you can use them to get what you want. However, your negative attitudes and beliefs may become obstacles to achieving your dream. For example, you may believe you can't have what you want, or you can only get a portion of it, or that getting what you want will create more problems, so it's better not to try. You might think that you're facing barriers you can't move beyond: your gender, your height, your lack of education, your work experience.

Attitudes and beliefs are never neutral. Whether yours are positive or negative, it's much more effective to deal with them

MY BELIEFS

Create a list about where you are and where you want to be with reference to your dream.

Category	My Beliefs About Where I Am Now	My Beliefs About Where I Want to Be
	_____	_____
	_____	_____
	_____	_____
	_____	_____
	_____	_____
	_____	_____
	_____	_____

now than later. Those opinions that are positive are your allies; they're "on your side" as you design the life you want. Those that are negative can sabotage you, especially if they're perceived as the biggest part of "where you are now," or if they get inserted into your dream.

Unexamined negative attitudes can become bigger than your dream, and turn into insurmountable obstacles after you're already on the road to what you want. If that happens, and you're stopped en route, you're unlikely to reach your dream.

Alternatively, negative attitudes and beliefs don't have to be as menacing as they may seem at first. Reexamine the Positioning Yourself exercise on pages 66–67, and note that each of your beliefs is just one of many components within a given area in the Where I Am Now column; no single one of your beliefs comprises the whole column. Confront and handle those attitudes now, and they can be used effectively to propel you toward where you want to be.

I am often asked how it's possible to get in touch with our beliefs, when it's widely known that people spend long periods in therapy to explore their deep-seated attitudes. In this process, you are looking at "what" are your attitudes and beliefs, rather than why you have them or where they came from. By the time most people reach this stage in the process of making dreams come true, they have little trouble voicing a wide range of attitudes and beliefs, particularly those that hold them back. Here's a roster of the ones I hear most frequently:

> I don't have the time, the money, the resources, the skills, the knowledge.
> I'm not successful enough, not good enough.
> I'm too successful, too young, too old, or too resistant to change, etc.
> I'm in the wrong geographical location.
> I don't have any knowledge in that area.
> I missed my opportunity years ago.
> It's not the right time.
> My energy is too low.
> It's too hard, too technical for me.
> I don't think I can learn what I need to know.
> I don't trust myself or anyone else.
> I worry about what others will think.
> I don't believe it's possible, so why bother?

In an uneven economy, the attitude I hear expressed most often is "I don't have the finances to handle it." Frequently, however, the very people who express reservations based on their finances are the ones who can't afford to stay where they are. From an economic perspective, they would benefit from making a change.

The important element is not that you have attitudes and

I *do* have the time, the money, the resources, the skills, the knowledge.

I'm successful enough, and good enough.

I'm old enough, young enough, and flexible enough.

I'm in a good geographical location.

I can accomplish this anywhere.

I have the knowledge in this new area.

I have a good opportunity before me now.

My energy is high.

I believe in me.

I can learn what I need to know.

I believe it's possible.

beliefs; it's how you use them. If you think you don't have the resources to get the job done, go back to the previous chapter's Positioning Yourself exercise and enter that belief into the Where I Am Now column. If you have a long list of attitudes and beliefs, the whole catalog belongs under the Where I Am Now column, whether the beliefs are positive or negative. In fact, interpreting something as a "good attitude" or a "bad attitude" doesn't make it good or bad. It's just an interpretation.

Do your beliefs empower or impede you? One day while working at my health club, I saw Greg. He was a handsome man, about age thirty-eight. He was staring off into space.

I jokingly said, "C'mon, aren't you here to work out? Get going!"

He said he was thinking about the year ahead and about some goals he had set.

"Like what?" I asked.

"I plan to be walking by the end of this year," he replied, as he crawled off a Nautilus machine and reached for the wheelchair I hadn't noticed. He explained that he had been in the wrong place at the wrong time, got caught in a crossfire, and was shot in the leg. His doctors thought it was a miracle that he lived through the night, and they told him and his family that he would never walk again.

However, one day, while Greg lay in a hospital bed feeling the futility of his situation, his toe moved. "It just moved," he told me. The doctors assured him it was "nothing," just nerves; but, for Greg, it was the beginning of a new belief. The expectation that he would walk again became the driving force of Greg's life, and he became passionately committed to turning his dream into reality.

I saw Greg recently. Not only was he walking, but he was eager to share his new dream. "My next step is to find myself a girlfriend and take her dancing. But my five-year goal is to run a marathon. Pretty unbelievable"—he chuckled—"for a guy who was told he would never walk again."

Whose beliefs are you buying? What's stopping you from going for your dreams? Anything and everything you want is no more than a belief away.

> *Your attitudes and beliefs*
> *either empower*
> *or impede you.*
> *They are never neutral.*

Interpretations

When something happens in any kind of situation, the results can be interpreted negatively or positively. Your interpretation depends on your attitudes and beliefs.

There are many ways to look at the same incident. An old Chinese story tells about a young man who falls off a horse and breaks his leg. Initially, everyone interpreted the incident as negative; then war broke out and the young man was unable to serve in the army because of his broken leg. Was the accident then good or bad?

If a member of your staff suddenly seems to be doing ineffective work, it could be interpreted as the employee's lack of interest and general unhappiness. On the other hand, maybe the employee is dealing with a problem at home, or is concerned about job stability. Which interpretation is correct? In this case, inaccurate interpretations can be avoided by communication. Ask the employee what's going on; create a dialogue so you don't have to guess about someone else's behavior.

You can learn to use interpretations to empower yourself by getting accurate information, and by thinking of outcomes in positive terms. If you believe there are opportunities in everything that happens, the possibilities will appear everywhere. If you take the attitude that you'll ''believe it when you see it,'' chances are you'll never see it. This is an important point; don't glide over it!

Here's how your beliefs can empower or impede you in moving toward your dream. If you are reacting to negative beliefs, they are obstacles and will trip you up or keep you from reaching your dream. However, if you use them as tools to help you achieve your dreams, you transform them into stepping stones. Now your beliefs have become the bridge that allows you to move easily from where you are to where you want to be. You decide. Will you use your beliefs as stumbling blocks or stepping stones?

Think about the old saying that you can see a glass as half full or half empty. How you see it is up to you. If you believe in yourself and trust that Magic will appear, you'll be training yourself to use the power of interpretation to get what you want as opposed to keeping you where you are.

Facing Fear

Imagine that there's a gift in your life, one that's so obvious that every time it shows up it's a direct sign that you're on the right path to getting what you want. Fear can be this gift, and this is how it works.

When our first parents were driven out of Paradise, Adam is believed to have remarked to Eve, "My dear, we live in an age of transition."
—W. C. Inge

Everyone's life is about change. Sometimes *you* change, and sometimes you change your life. Often, when you think you have everything figured out, something happens, and significant parts of your life are altered. Some people fear change, some people resist change, and some people claim to thrive on it.

Human beings seem devoted to consistency as a way of life. Yet the only constant is change. What you fear may not revolve around what is being changed; what you call "fear" and associate with a negative belief may simply be your body's resistance to the act of changing.

You can learn whether you're on the right path to where you want to be by facing fear and acknowledging it as a landmark for change. That's the gift. If you were not moving away from your current identity, if you were not seeking to change your life, you would not be experiencing fear.

Because we think of "change" as filled with murky unknowns, the ultimate fear may feel like death. However, the experience is actually the old you dying away, and allowing you to be transformed. This is good news. By trusting what you want, often you will be able to release the part of you that was

What would you
attempt to do
if you knew you
could not fail?
—Dr. Robert Schuller

afraid of making your dream come true. By shedding the pieces that no longer fit, you can create a new dream to move toward. Fear is actually a measurement tool; it means that you're leaving the old behind; it's a gift that indicates you are closer to your dream.

Empowering Yourself Out of Fear

Fear can be seen as a healthy and natural mechanism, a sign of vitality, and evidence that you are in process. Sadly, unless you learn to use fear as empowerment, it can also stop your progress.

First, you need to distinguish fear that protects from fear that restricts. When fear keeps you out of dark alleys at two o'clock in the morning, obviously listen to your inner voice. On the other hand, fear of change, fear of moving closer to a dream, or fear of something that you've always wanted is negative and limiting.

Suppose you always wanted a little country home. You've dreamed about the rooms, the yard, the picket fence. One day, you find your dream home and you think, "Omigod, now what?" The thoughts that fly through your mind create fear, and you invent stories to justify why you're afraid.

"I just can't give up my friends and move away."

"I'll never sell my house."

"It's too small or too large for me."

---

*If you see opportunities
in everything that
happens, possibilities
appear everywhere.*

"The commute will be too far."

"No one will visit me out there."

"It was only a dream anyway."

Take a fresh look at the dream. Start by closing your eyes and reconnecting with the dream house. Assume there are no limiting circumstances like the ones listed above, and ask, "Is this the house of my dreams?" If the answer is "No," you can let it go. If the answer is "Yes," then you can go for it.

It's actually possible to use fear as a way of getting something that you want. On page 81, you can catch up with Carol, whose story began in chapter 1, to learn how she used fear to launch her dream of running her own dance company.

You may think that Carol's experience is too neat an ending to her story. Maybe you know about someone who's afraid and is unable to devise a powerful solution. Part of having a belief includes wanting the situation to turn out in a certain way; and, often, fear is used to justify the outcome.

Whether or not the situation will conclude as you believe it will, what matters is the meaning you give to the outcome. Will a negative result mean that you're a failure and that you shouldn't go for your dream, or will you be able to accept the

---

THIS SPACE AVAILABLE FOR YOUR DREAMS.

---

outcome, whatever it is, and keep going? Accepting the conse-
quences, good or bad, will free you; take a risk, but be aware that
things sometimes turn out differently than you expected.

In Carol's case, facing her fear enabled her to deal with it. If
her plan had not worked out, she would have developed another; confronting her fear was empowering.

Thoughts and Feelings

Earlier I mentioned that attitudes and beliefs lead to thoughts
and feelings, which in turn lead to decisions and choices. If you
want to become aware of your attitudes and beliefs, pay attention to what you're thinking and feeling. When you can hear
your beliefs in your head, you can transform your life. They no
longer sneak up on you. You hear your limiting beliefs, but they
no longer stop you. Remember:

Attitudes & Beliefs

< create >

Thoughts & Feelings

< which create >

Choices & Decisions

If your dream is to establish a new career, but your belief is
that it's not possible, what do you think and feel about that? Do
you feel futility? Have you resigned youself to the idea that you
can't have your dream? Or do you think you can have what you
want because you deserve it?

Suppose your dream is to be famous. Specifically, you want
USA Today to write a front-page story about you, but you don't
believe it's possible. The logical sequence of your thought process might be that you don't think it can happen so you decide
not to pursue it.

Now you have the same dream with a different belief. You
believe it's possible to make your dream come true. Your thought

> # Keep speaking your dream, keep speaking the possibility.

process is "I think I can make this happen," and "I think I know who can help me." Your new choice is to go for it.

Simply changing your belief has shifted your internal conversation from thinking of your dream as impossible to seeing its possibilities. This is an example of removing the obstacles in order to let the Magic happen. We are back to the basic formula for making your dream come true.

REAL PEOPLE: CAROL

Carol, who wanted to become the full-time executive director of her own dance company, feared severing her ties with the people at her current place of employment. She'd been working

> # When you can hear your beliefs in your head, you can transform your life.

there for a long time and had developed relationships that mattered to her. She believed that if she left, the relationships would be over. That belief was somehow turned into a fear that she was going to be alone in her new venture.

When Carol clarified where she wanted to be, she decided to take her relationships with her. She also realized that one of her skills, writing grant proposals in the field of the arts, was something she could sell to the company for which she'd been working.

Carol approached her employer and suggested that his company become Carol's client; her employer, seeing the value in hiring someone on a project-by-project basis, accepted Carol's proposal. Because she assumed a new role, that of free-lancer, the project was awarded to Carol on her own terms. She negotiated more money, better hours, and greater flexibility than she'd had as the company's employee.

Without announcing her fears, Carol was able to use them as a mechanism for getting her employer to "go with her." The important aspect of this is that Carol identified her fears to herself, and developed a way to deal with them that catapulted her dream into reality.

Carol also saw that she had been using her fear for a long time to stop herself from moving forward. There was a gap between where she was and where she wanted to be, and that gap was created by her beliefs. When she examined her attitudes honestly, she was able to use them to break through and move toward what she wanted. In fact, she wound up with more than she thought she could have: she didn't just walk away from her employer feeling okay about it; she walked away with a new client, and a powerful relationship with her former boss.

You will find it easier to become aware of your thoughts and feelings now that you're clear about your attitudes and beliefs. It's even possible, once you understand that you have a core belief, to go back and change it. If you alter your beliefs, your

> *When you identify your fears and learn to use them positively, you can develop ways to deal with them that will catapult your dream into reality.*

thoughts and feelings will change, too. Your changed thoughts and feelings, in turn, will motivate you to examine your decisions and choices. What are the decisions you're making in your life? Are they positive choices that will move you toward your dream, or are your decisions moving you away from things you don't want?

Perhaps your dream is to move from the East Coast to California, or from California to New York, but you fear that such a move would be too far away from your family. That feeling may refer back to an attitude or belief that your family won't love you if they don't see you. Is this belief real? This is a good question to ask yourself about all your beliefs, because the truth is that beliefs are not real. They are something we have created and we hold to be true. We have the power to re-create them at any time. Do you believe this? Notice your belief about changing your beliefs.

You can change your attitude by adopting the belief that you can have it all, including friends all over the world. The new outlook will help you understand that wherever you're living, family and friends will come to visit you, or you can visit them, and that you'll make new friends easily. Thus, you have adopted a positive feeling about yourself and your place in the world; then, if you decide that California is it, making the choice will be easy.

Some people think it's difficult to change a belief and some people think it's easy; that's just your *belief about your beliefs*. If you have a belief that is getting in your way and is crying out to be changed, the Big Book of Your Beliefs exercise, below, can help you do it.

Your attitudes and beliefs can work to empower you or to frustrate you. By confronting doubt and fear, you will allow the Magic to show up. Magic cannot live where doubt reigns. You need to believe—in yourself and in your dreams. Then the Magic will come and you can make decisions and choices that support making your dreams come true. When you let the Magic in, more Magic will come.

THE BIG BOOK OF YOUR BELIEFS

Place yourself in a quiet spot and relax. Take several deep breaths and prepare yourself for the journey into your mind.

Imagine that you're in the attic of your mind. It's filled with lots of dusty memories: your bicycle from when you were three, your mother's wedding dress, old albums.

As you walk through the attic, you come to a corner. In the corner there's a beautiful pedestal on top of which is a big book. On the cover of the book it says, "My Beliefs." Blow a little dust off the book, open it, and turn to a page where you have a belief that you want to change.

See your belief on that page. You can write in the space below or just picture it in your mind. Whatever that old belief is, read it, and prepare to change it.

Perhaps you believe it's not possible to have what you want.

Read that belief from the page in the book, take a big, black Magic Marker, and draw a huge *X* through it. Then see yourself tear the page out of the book and burn it. Get rid of that belief: cross it out, tear it out, and burn it. Feel the emotion of finally letting this old belief go.

My limiting belief that is stopping me from having my dream come true is:

_____

_____

_____

_____

_____

Now you're left with a clean page in the book. Pick up a Magic Marker in your favorite color and write your new belief. Your new belief will correspond to the one you burned, but it will be stated positively and in the first person: ``It is possible for me to have what I want.'' Consider adding the word ``easily.''

Write your new belief expressively and with flair, so that you feel it, and you can internalize it. After you've written it, read your new belief out loud to yourself. Then close the book, leave the attic, and know that your new, positive attitude now lives in The Big Book of Your Beliefs.

My wonderful new belief is:

_____

_____

_____

Do you believe you changed your belief? Do you believe at least that it's possible you changed it? Or do you believe it can't be that easy? What if it is that easy? It's all up to you. You decide whether to believe or not. That's how beliefs work.

Practice believing your new belief.

THE "C" WORD— COMMITMENT

Never, never, never, never give up.
—Sir Winston Churchill

Now that you have determined where you are and where you want to be, you'll have to make a choice. Do you feel a greater commitment to having more of the same or to having your dream come true?

Many people find that once they get to the commitment stage, dramatic things happen. The continuation of some of the Real People stories, found at the end of this chapter, illustrates not only how people move into the commitment stage, but also how the Magic shows up once the commitment is made.

A priority question to ask is what kind of commitment you're willing to make to achieve your dream. The answer may surprise you, just as the Carters were surprised that they wanted to close the business to which they thought they were devoted. However, once you are committed to making your dream come true, everything seems to move faster, and you seem to know with greater certainty how you need to proceed. Your next step becomes evident, as does the step after that.

I sometimes refer to "commitment" as the "C" word, because a lot of people think of it as if it were an obscenity. Perhaps they view commitment as "locking them in" or "getting stuck." When I speak of commitment, I mean a covenant with yourself and for yourself; committing to something that you want, to having your dream come true, to moving forward.

Until one is committed, there is hesitancy, the chance to draw back, always ineffectiveness, concerning all acts of initiative (and creation). There is one elementary truth the ignorance of which kills countless ideas and splendid plans: that the moment one definitely commits oneself, then providence moves too. All sorts of things occur to help one that would never otherwise have occurred. A whole stream of events issues from the decision, raising in one's favor all manner of unforeseen incidents and meetings and material assistance which no one could have dreamed would have come their way. Whatever you can do or dream you can, begin it. Boldness has *genius, power* and *magic* in it. Begin it now.
—Johann Wolfgang von Goethe

Commitment is hardly a dirty word; on the contrary, it's a powerful experience.

Nevertheless, there are some common attitudes and beliefs that stop people from making a commitment to themselves:

"It's going to force my hand."

"I'll be stuck with it and won't be able to change direction later."

"It might be the wrong move, and if I keep my options open, something better will show up."

"I might look silly."

"It will take longer for me to get there than I care to invest."

"I might not be able to do what I say."

"I might not be able to follow through."

"What if I fail?"

You can deal with "commitment" in a similar manner to the way in which you treated "fear" in chapter 7: you can redefine commitment as something positive, a tool that can be used to propel you toward having your dream. Maybe what you've always needed to reach your dream was to have $2,000; commit to accumulating that sum by a certain date so you can put yourself into action. Commitment is a much more powerful way of living than waiting around and hoping.

Walk Your Talk

A critical element of commitment is doing what you say you're going to do, actually being as good as your word. It's "walking your talk."

Right now, your dream doesn't exist in reality. It begins to take on life as you envision it and speak about it. During the commitment stage, as you open yourself up to unlimited possibilities, many things can start to happen. If you're not responsible about your commitment, the process will start to unravel and you will undermine yourself and your dream. Get into the practice of following through on your commitment: walk your talk.

When you live your commitment, a new dynamic will start to show up, bringing opportunities you didn't know were possible. Be especially careful at this point to avoid being stopped by

> ``It's going to open up
> new possibilities.''
>
> ``Life is full of choices. I chose it.''
>
> ``It might be a good move,
> and by staying committed, other
> good things will show up.''
>
> ``It won't take long for me
> to get there.''
>
> ``I may do exactly what I say.''
>
> ``I will be able to follow through.''
>
> ``I intend to succeed.''

limiting beliefs and attitudes; sometimes in the commitment phase, self-sabotage can "sneak up" on you when you're least expecting it.

For example, you might be committed to doing something even though you're worried about not having the time or money to do it. Don't stop acting because of your concern. By living in the commitment, you open up opportunities—perhaps some new resource that will make the whole thing feasible. You might say that, if you are willing to make the commitment down to the marrow in your bones, the stars will line up in the heavens and the Magic will show up in your life.

The Sliding Glass Door exercise following will help you learn to live in your commitment. When the exercise has been completed, you may decide not to commit and step through the door. That's fine. Be clear that this side of the glass door is where you choose to be right now. Your dream will always be there on the other side of the Sliding Glass Door. When you're ready, reach out, open the door, make the commitment, and step through.

Once you do, rate your Passion Level. It will probably be quite high. Good work!

THE SLIDING GLASS DOOR

Remove yourself from outside distractions by putting yourself someplace where you won't be disturbed. Relax. Take a few deep breaths. This exercise is completely about you, about stepping into your commitment.

Imagine that you're standing with your nose pressed against a glass door, so close to it that your breath is steaming up the glass. As you wipe away the steam, you see a beautiful place on the other side of the glass. Rainbows, waterfalls, beautiful animals, heaven on earth, Nirvana.

Feel your feet standing on the floor on your side of the glass door, the other side of Nirvana. You're standing in the ''Where I Am Now,'' where you live with everything that's happening in your life, including your attitudes and beliefs. Looking through the glass door, you can see the beauty on the other side. You will have the opportunity to find out if the other side is a place where you want to be.

Grasp the handle and slide the door open. A gentle, warm breeze comes wafting in, and there's a delicious smell in the air. You feel warm and welcome.

As you gaze around, you see everything on the other side that you want, everything that's in your dream, everything you're committed to having. If you choose, your family is there, too, your friends, your dream house, your dream life. All the elements of your dream are there, on the other side of the door.

Notice where you are and where you want to be. All you need to do to get to the other side is make the commitment and step through.

Ask yourself, ``Is this what I want? Will I commit to this?'' If the answer is ``Yes,'' lift your foot and step through.

Now you're on the other side, living in a land of possibilities. Here's where the Magic can happen, where all your dreams can come true. Don't worry if you don't have it all figured out. Just trust: now that you're standing in your commitment, you're standing in your dream.

Take a couple of deep breaths and relax.

REAL PEOPLE: THE CARTERS

The Carters, the couple who owned their own store, were committed to having a successful business. They were surprised to learn that their retail operation, to which they had been devoted, was not the kind of success they wanted.

When they understood that where they were wasn't even close to where they wanted to be, the Carters realized that they had to make a decision: did they want more of the same, or were they ready to make a commitment to having their dream? When they decided to live on purpose and move forward with their dream, they did it in a big way. They closed their store and transformed their whole business, to say nothing of their lives, into something else.

Because Magic happens in commitment, things started to change for the Carters. When they recognized how central their

PASSION SCALE

Place an *X* next to the area that best describes your level of passion about your commitment. Do it right now.

_____Red-hot
_____Turned on
_____Excited
_____Very interested
_____Interested
_____Some possibility
_____No interest

relationship was to each of them, they committed to creating a shared goal out of their individual Purposes. Thus, an unexpected outcome was that they became more committed to each other.

The Carters' commitment got them into immediate action. Within three months, they had phased out their retail operation, and created a new consulting business that gave them greater flexibility and the opportunity to be in closer partnership with each other.

REAL PEOPLE: NANCY

Nancy, the woman starting a new business at the same time she was pregnant with her first baby, was committed to having balance in her life. For Nancy, that meant having quality time for her husband and baby, and also for her new business.

The issue wasn't about only balancing time; it also was about balancing energy so she would have enough to give to both areas of her life. Nancy's commitment was to be the best that she could be personally and professionally, without selling out.

Everybody has only twenty-four hours in each day, and Nancy began to think about how she was going to use her allotted time to achieve her dream. Once she understood her commitment clearly, the steps she needed to take became obvious.

Nancy decided that she was only going to work a certain number of days during the week. She built a lot of flexibility into that decision by allowing herself to choose weekly which days that would be. She did not see her overall commitment to her business as amorphous, but she allowed herself to be accommodating in the way she made it work.

She also knew she would need some help to achieve the flexibility she wanted, and she immediately hired a live-in housekeeper. That relieved her both of the concern about child

---

Commitment leads to action. Action brings your dream closer.

---

care while she was at the office and of the need to perform household chores. Thus, when Nancy came home from her new business, she had the time and energy to be with her family. Her commitment to her dreams enabled her to create a balanced life, one that she chose deliberately and loved living.

Commitment comes in many different forms. It's up to you.

YES, IT'S POSSIBLE—
A RALLYING CRY

You see things and say, "why?"
But I dream things that never were and I say,
"why not?"
—George Bernard Shaw

We began this book speaking about "possibility" as something you can have. In this chapter, you get to play with your dream as if you truly believe that it is possible to have what you're committed to, to have all the goals in your life align, to have a life you love, to have the time to enjoy it, and to start right now.

"Possibility" is my favorite word, a whole new way of being. Having possibility in your life requires that you practice speaking the words "It is possible" and believing them at every opportunity. Unfortunately, most of us have been trained to believe that the things we want are not possible. To change that takes retraining. You can learn to hear yourself, and you can educate those around you to hear the possibility in what you say, instead of saying "Have you lost your mind?"

The assumption that "it is possible" is at the core of having your dream come true. If you have read this far in the book and you confess that you don't believe you can have your dream, confront and handle your negative beliefs before you go on. You may wish to go back and read some of the earlier chapters to identify what's holding you back and how it can be changed. *You can't make your dream come true if you don't believe it's possible.*

The Sliding Glass Door exercise, found in chapter 8, is one of the methods you can employ here. On this side of the door is your belief that it's not possible, but the other side is filled with possibilities. Notice where you're standing: are you on this side, in "I don't believe it's possible," or are you on the other side, standing in your commitment? Choose one.

You can even suspend your negative attitude and say, "I'll believe it for a while and give it a shot." However, I recommend that you walk through that door. Be committed to having your dream come true, be willing to have it be possible, allow your attitudes and beliefs to support you, and stop holding on to some outdated negative opinion. Step through; that's where the Magic will happen. Remember that possibility leads to Magic, and Magic means producing extraordinary results. Without possibility, there's no Magic. When you allow the Magic, there are many opportunities to handle all of your concerns and to help move you to the next step.

Moving into Your Project

Possibility begins to seem likely when you move forward from dreams to projects. As you start to involve yourself in the specific, measurable results, the dream will become animated and

> *What today is impossible*
> *to do, but if it could*
> *be done, would*
> *fundamentally change*
> *what I do?*
> *—Joel Barker*

YOUR DREAM IS POSSIBLE.

take on credibility. If you don't know how to accomplish that, relax; we'll outline how to make it happen.

When you've made your commitment, you will have a different perspective on your dream than you did when you were wondering if it would ever happen. Maybe you once thought you didn't have the time to go after that new piece of business that you want; now that you're committed to doing it, and you've dealt with all your negative attitudes and beliefs, you may see the logic of freeing time by giving up something that doesn't interest you anymore. Your new outlook, that it makes sense to give up something that no longer has value to *you*, or passion for you, is a direct result of your ability to see where you are, compared to where you want to be. How much extra time might you have if you started saying ''No, thank you'' to the things that you don't have to do and that you're not passionate about? Imagine filling some of that ''spare'' time with things that really matter to you, things that you choose because you simply want to do them.

Refocusing on your Life's Purpose (who you are and what turns you on) will assist you in deciding when to give up or walk away from something. You'll notice a lighter, freer feeling as you let go of the old and create room to embrace the new.

Living in your commitment also allows for the possibility of a new relationship or partnership, or a means of connecting resources in a creative way that you hadn't considered before. You don't yet have to focus on the specific strategies and tactics; look at what else you might put into your dream to have everything you want. Your new commitment may even lead you to include items you didn't know or think about earlier.

For example, in defining your dream now, you might say, "I want an understanding, lucrative, supportive partner." Or "I will discover a venture capital firm that's interested in funding my project." Perhaps you're ready to brainstorm with other people; now that you see your dream clearly and you're committed to having it, you can gather a group of individuals whom you respect, and who can help you decide on the specifics.

Maybe you previously determined that you wanted to live in a particular location, and now you want to put some flesh on that bare-bones dream: a particular kind of house, a pool or Jacuzzi, walk-in closets in which you can see your designer wardrobe. Have fun with your dream as you expand it.

Possibility also appears when you want to create balance in your life. You begin to see, as Nancy did, that you can be successful in business and still have time to be with your family; that, once you set aside your negative attitudes and beliefs, you can allow yourself to have somebody else cook dinner or help make your life easier in some other way.

The important question, now and always, is "What else is possible?" At the end of this chapter, you will find the continuing story of the Carters, who found many possibilities once they began to live in their commitment. Nancy, the expectant mother with the new business, discovered such possibilities as working fewer days and having live-in help. For Carol, the woman who started the dance company, the possibilities were to write grant proposals as a free-lancer, to provide other kinds of consulting services, and to raise sponsorship dollars for her new venture.

WHAT ELSE IS POSSIBLE?

DO NOT SKIP THIS PAGE; DO NOT SKIP THIS EXERCISE.
When you think you've listed everything that's possible, and you're sure there's nothing left, ask yourself once again, "What else is possible?" I assure you more will come.

What else is possible? _____
_____
_____
_____

What else is possible? _____
_____
_____
_____

What else is possible? _____
_____
_____
_____

What else is possible? _____
_____
_____
_____

On page 100 you will find an exercise that will help you ask yourself, "What else is possible?" Do not skip What Else Is Possible? It will help to ensure that you have included in your dream all the pieces you truly want.

Another exercise to help you see what else is possible is called the Looking Back exercise, page 102. Project yourself out in your mind's eye *one year from today.* Looking back from that point, write out how the last year "was" for you. Remember who you are now: someone standing in your Life's Purpose, whose dreams are deliberately chosen, who has a clear sense of where you are and where you want to be, and who has removed all the limiting beliefs and obstacles.

Through the Looking Back exercise, you can develop a game plan by projecting yourself into the future to look back at the past. You can also understand the feelings and sensations of those events that are *about* to unfold in your life. Because you have become so focused and directed, the high probability is that, over the next year, you will live out your projection.

As you begin to live what you projected, the Magic will start to show up. Be specific when you're "looking back." State your "accomplishments" during the last year. Draw the complete picture for yourself, leaving out none of the details. Remember, you stepped through the Sliding Door.

What were you passionate about?
Where did your achievements take place?
Who else was involved?
What funds became available?
How did you spend the extra money that came your way?
How did others respond?
How did you feel as you passed certain milestones?
How did going down one path take you to another?
Who did you meet this year that you've always wanted to meet?

LOOKING BACK ON *THIS* YEAR

How this year was for me (if everything was possible):

It's now _____ (Date—one year from today).

During this last year, I_____

_____

_____

_____

_____

_____

_____

_____

_____

_____

_____

_____

_____

_____

_____

How did you spend your exotic vacation?

How did you look and feel?

How was that last year for you, now that you made your dream come true?

Let more and more come to you as you're writing; you'll be surprised at how much detail you will have about the "past" year.

Everything up to this point—all the exercises, visualizations, writings—has been a projection of what you want to have. Now we will transform it all into projects with specific, measurable results. This is where all your possibilities and dreams will begin to become part of your reality, and where your passion will start to live powerfully in the present.

REAL PEOPLE: THE CARTERS

The Carters began to see the possibilities as soon as they made their commitment to sell the retail computer store and pursue their dreams. First, they realized they could have a whole new consulting business serving clients with whom they had done business before. Second, they determined that their retail business could be sold to someone who would continue to serve their previous customers. Third, the new owner agreed to refer to the Carters retail customers who needed consultation about purchases made at the store.

In other words, they took their dream to a new level by evolving a new relationship. Rather than separating themselves completely from their previous business, they found a way to make a profitable connection for their new business.

Of course, there were some obstacles to overcome. The Carters

> # Wasn't this coming year a great year?

had many attitudes and beliefs about closing the store: they couldn't see how they were going to continue serving their clients. They thought that closing the store meant they had failed.

Once they went through the process, they were able to turn their negative attitudes and beliefs around, and use them to propel themselves toward their dream. When they knew with clarity what they wanted, and that they were committed to having it, the next steps became evident: they scheduled the closing of the store, they set a date by which the new business would be set up, and they got into action. Setting the date made the commitment tangible and moved their dream into the project phase, the subject of the next chapter.

All that we see or
seem is but a dream
within a dream.
—Edgar Allan Poe

PROJECTS THAT MOVE YOU FORWARD

If you have built castles in the air, your work
need not be lost; that is where they should be.
Now put the foundations under them.
—Henry David Thoreau

In chapter 4, you chose a specific area of your life to work on to simplify the process of learning the techniques in this book. You've been developing your dream in that area, going up the Passion Pyramid, opening up more and more possibilities about your dream. In this chapter, you will learn how to turn your dream into a project with specific, measurable results. The action of doing so will make your dream begin to exist in your life, not just in your head or on paper. This is where your passion becomes powerful.

Remember that everything comes from Purpose. Standing in your Purpose, ask, with respect to the area you selected, "What dream do I have that I can turn into an exciting project?" Then look for what needs to be added to your project to get it scheduled into your life—a date, a person, a number.

For instance, if your dream is to travel, your project might be to go on a cruise this year. If you don't yet know where you want to go, but you know the locale is exotic, open an atlas, pick a specific place and begin to arrange your trip.

My own Life's Purpose is to joyously self-express and my personal dream is to travel the world in style and elegance; my project is to book an exotic cruise by a specific date.

Of course, there are many ways to travel the world in style and

Dreams come alive
through projects
with specific,
measurable results.

elegance. Other projects that could come from my Purpose and my dream might be to travel first-class five times this year; to attend at least three formal events in cities outside my hometown; to fly in a private jet plane at least once during the next six months; to spend three months abroad living in a beautiful place at the ocean.

You don't have to limit yourself to one project; all you have to do is make sure that all your projects are part of your dream. When I develop projects for my professional dream—integrating more playtime into my work—I can change things around, as long as everything remains aligned with my Purpose and my professional dream. Thus, I might create a project that would allow me to continue my work while visiting Europe. Note that I only have to create the project at this point; I don't have to limit the possibilities by figuring out how I'm going to do it. We'll get to that.

Ellen, whose Purpose was to have a life filled with fun and adventure, had a well-being goal called "To Live a Spa Life." She created a project called "Go to an Elegant Spa at Least Four Times a Year, Each Time for at Least One Week's Duration." She didn't yet have any of it planned—financially, logistically, or time-wise—but once she created the project, it took on life and became part of her reality.

Some projects are easy: you merely have to schedule them into your calendar. To get into action on her dream, Ellen developed a simple project to get two facials and two massages each month. She also requested literature from Cal-A-Vie, a world-class spa near San Diego. She hung it on her office wall to keep her dream near and in view and soon scheduled a week of pure pleasure and pampering for herself. Other projects may be more complicated, and require a well-thought-out plan to get there.

A project has to be specific, but it can deal with any aspect of your life: Brian created a project to raise $25,000 so his foundation could open for business. The only criterion for a project is that it come from the bottom up on the Passion Pyramid— meaning that it's an expression of your Purpose and your dream —and that it be specific and measurable. What is a project that you could make up or create that would get you in action on your dream, either a piece of your dream or the entire thing?

Synchronicity

Synchronicity may be a fun, new way for you to think about having your dream. Before reading this book, you may have thought about your dream as something you might—or might not—ever have. Now, you've expanded your possibilities and allowed for more opportunities to create projects for reaching your dream.

When you look at the whole picture of your dream, you will see that some of the areas overlap. The overlap will enable you to handle something in one area of your life that automatically takes care of something in another area. This is called synchronicity.

When I was in college, my goals were so interwoven that the substance of many of my courses overlapped. There were times that I could write one term paper and, with slight modifications, use it for three different classes. The point of having Magic in your life is to make it easier to make your dreams come true. If you

> *Synchronicity:*
> *when things start to*
> *happen at the right time,*
> *flow together easily,*
> *and work interchangeably.*

stand in your Purpose and look at the broad picture of your dream, it's possible to get what you want while simplifying your life.

New possibilities will become available as you develop projects and get into action on them. Opportunities that you couldn't have seen before will start to look like they have potential. Of course, you might be stymied by an old attitude or belief. If you are, ask yourself whether you're still committed to your dreams; if the answer is "Yes," stay committed. As long as your projects come from your Purpose and are aligned with your dreams, as long as you still feel the passion, stay in action.

> *You have no idea*
> *what kind of Magic*
> *could be waiting for you*
> *right around the bend,*
> *on the other side of the*
> *place where you got stuck.*

Throughout this book, for the sake of simplicity, we have focused on your dreams in one area of your life. However, the intention of the process is that you will master the techniques of consciously designing your entire life. Once you learn the procedure—and you can only learn it by practicing—you'll find it easy to map it into all the other areas of your life.

The only files I maintain in my office are files relating to my projects. Everything else has been cleared away. As my project files grow, they open onto more projects, and sometimes new projects develop within an existing one. There's a great deal of overlap because one of my dreams is to integrate my personal and professional life. That doesn't mean I'm a workaholic; it means that I've created work that expresses who I am in the world, and I can combine my work with the rest of my life, easily and joyfully. This is bliss.

Thus, to accomplish my personal project of integrating my love of traveling in style with my desire to speak publicly about something that has a positive impact, I created a project called "Going Abroad Speaking About Making Dreams Come True." Since I created the project, I have been invited to do a thirty-country speaking tour for the World Association of Women Entrepreneurs. It all started with my dream, and then it seemed to fall into place effortlessly.

Aligning Goals to Support Your Dream

Let's recap what you've accomplished thus far. Standing in your Purpose, you have created dreams in at least one aspect of your life. You've stepped through the Sliding Glass Door and you're on the other side, where there is everything you desire and are committed to having in your life in this chosen area. Now go back and have a look at the other areas of your life to ensure that they line up with your dream.

As you create a project, if you find a dream that seems inconsistent or incompatible—perhaps you're worried that you're selling out in one situation in order to have another—check to see whether your "concern" is real, or whether it's a negative attitude or belief. For example, if the hours you've designated for your project add up to more than twenty-four each day, you have an inconsistency. On the other hand, if they add up to six or eight and you're still troubled about having enough time for everything, acknowledge that the issue comes from an old belief. Then make a commitment that you will use your time in support of having your dream.

Look at your life holistically; all of the components, including the dreams, are—or need to be—working parts of your life. Get a picture of it as a whole; perhaps there's a piece that's missing, that would tie things together to give you more time and flexibility, to make your life easier.

During the Sliding Glass Door exercise, one of my clients became very emotional. "I can't step through," she claimed.

When I asked why not, she explained there was no ground, no foundation. "Well, put it in," I said. With the foundation in place, she could step through the door.

We later saw that her dream—to make some radical changes in her business—was a big stretch from where she was. When she realized the emotional difficulty her employees were having with her new plans, she began to lay the proper groundwork with them to make a smooth transition.

Align your dreams by eliminating any inconsistencies.

What are your visualizations telling you? What's missing from your life that, if in place, would make your life easier?

I'm not torn between my personal and professional aspects; they are both me. I give myself plenty of time to relax and play, so when I go away on vacation I often do it in a barter situation: perhaps I offer a workshop in exchange for a week at a resort. Trading my services takes into consideration many of my dreams: my professional dream of having work that I love and that expresses who I am in the world; my personal dream of being with creative visionaries to produce results that have an impact; my well-being dream of being emotionally, mentally, spiritually, and physically balanced. The bartering opportunity never existed before I became clear about what I wanted and what I was committed to; now it exists regularly, and it ties together many of the aspects of my life.

A question that often comes up is how you identify the area you may have missed, the very one that may give you the complete arsenal of tools you need to make your dreams come true. Go back to the Passion Pyramid and look at your Life's Purpose. Then look at all the dreams you have determined you want in every aspect of your life.

This is not an exercise in creating more work for yourself. Rather, by asking yourself during the alignment process what you may not have seen before as a possibility, you will simplify your life and allow yourself to see the possibilities now. A growing number of people find that what's missing is not necessarily tangible; they need more space, more time, or some other personal resource.

Do you want to be more relaxed because you will feel better if you stop taking it all so seriously?

Did you leave out enough recreational time, or time simply to breathe and to be?

Is there a volunteer effort or another contribution you want to make?

Ask yourself:

*What would make
your life easier?*

*What would make your
life take on a glow?*

*What would give you
more time, more fun,
more excitement?*

You don't necessarily have to create another project to accomplish these things; perhaps you can save yourself time and energy by linking together two or more of the projects you've already identified. Think positively; you are designing a new life for yourself. Rather than formulating a dream that's stated in the negative, such as "Remove some of the clutter," develop instead a dream that supports your having more space or time, freedom or flexibility.

I discovered that what was missing for me was to have work that I love. Just plugging that one piece into my dream enabled me to begin developing projects that I savor. For example, it had never occurred to me before that going on a cruise or to a spa was a way of making money or being successful in business. That

> # You can be doing work that you love to do.

possibility showed up when I included the element of having work that I love, and saw that I could tie it together with my other dreams. I realized that I could flourish and take better care of myself while spending less time and energy than I had before. The more of yourself that you have, the more you can put into your projects, which are a way for you to pro-ject your dreams into the world.

If you want to live every day with passion, design a project that's bigger than your life, one that you don't know how to accomplish. Don't create a project "out of the blue"; develop one out of your Purpose as you would any other project. My bigger-than-life project is that by the time I die, people will be speaking about dreams in a completely new way, as if their dreams are something that absolutely can be had by a specific day. When you speak to me about your dreams, be prepared to pull out your calendar. I'm interested in getting you into action to make your dreams come true.

I'm not yet certain how to fulfill my bigger-than-life project, but it turns me on and gets me into great conversations with people. Remember, my dream is to partner with creative vision-aries to produce impactful results. Speaking with people about their dreams allows everyone to show up as a visionary, to be turned on and excited about their possibilities.

I don't allow myself to be stopped by the fact that I haven't figured out how to accomplish my bigger-than-life project. I move on by developing strategies and tactics, by scheduling it into my life and letting the Magic happen. And it does. You'll read more about big dreams in the Dare to Dream Big section in chapter 17.

To keep yourself updated on your progress moving up the Passion Pyramid, reenter your Purpose, rewrite your dream, and indicate in the designated area on the Pyramid the project you created during this chapter. Make sure you are excited about your project and the possibilities it provides.

THE PASSION PYRAMID

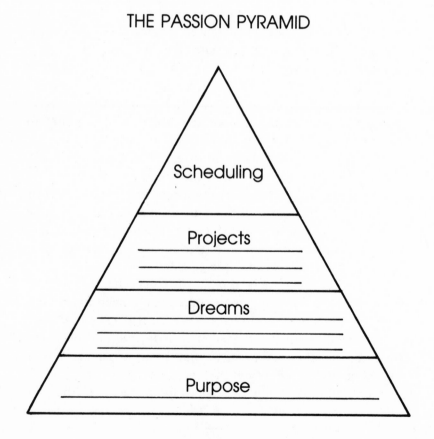

Remember, your Purpose is what turns you on; from that you created dreams that fulfill your Purpose; then you developed a project or several projects that represent your dream. Check in by rating yourself on the Passion Scale.

If you have created something that doesn't turn you on, change it. Develop a different project. If it all lines up and you're excited, even a little nervous about how you're going to make it happen, let's move on to doing it!

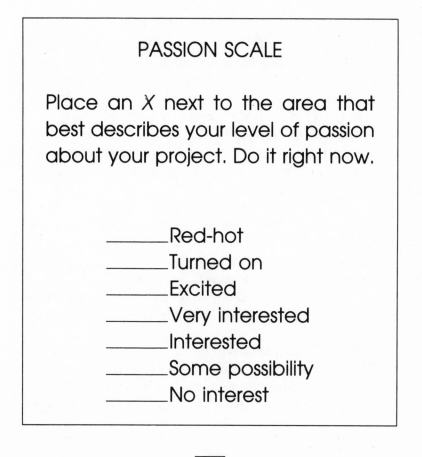

PASSION SCALE

Place an X next to the area that best describes your level of passion about your project. Do it right now.

_____Red-hot

_____Turned on

_____Excited

_____Very interested

_____Interested

_____Some possibility

_____No interest

STRATEGIES AND TACTICS
—BEING IN ACTION

"How do you eat an elephant?"
"One bite at a time."
—*Chinese proverb*

Now that you know what your project is, all you have to do is figure out how you're going to make it happen! There are multiple ways of completing any project or achieving any end result. To make your project part of your reality, you will need strategies and tactics to guide you toward your dream.

A strategy is the approach you take to achieve your dream. Tactics are the specific step-by-step items to accomplish the strategy. Sometimes, when an entire project is put on a "to do" list, the project is actually composed of four or five separate tactics; if the separate tasks aren't listed individually, the project may never happen. When you get clear about the project, as you did in the last chapter, you can explore the strategies and tactics you will need to accomplish it.

For example, I decided to create a project called "Go on at Least One Free and Fun Cruise to an Exotic Place Within the Next Three Months." Then I listed the ways I could make it happen.

In this case, I couldn't have chosen to purchase a ticket for a cruise, because my project was to go on a free cruise. It's important to be clear about the language you use to accomplish your commitment. One set of strategies might be needed to go on a fun cruise, while a different set is required to go on a free and fun cruise.

Other strategies I could have chosen include finding someone who would pay for my trip, or entering a contest to win a free cruise. I chose to create a bartering relationship by booking my workshop on a cruise ship in return for a free trip.

The tactics to accomplish the strategy were clear: list and describe some topics about which I could speak; prepare a biography; get the name and number of several cruise ship lines that might be interested in such an arrangement. I decided to focus my energy on a certain cruise ship, rather than mass-mailing my proposal: I wanted the best cruise I could find, so I committed to getting booked by Cunard Lines, which owns the luxury liner *Queen Elizabeth II*.

Because I was passionate about what I was doing, I was living in a world of possibility, and I was feeling powerful about accomplishing the results. I was definitely in action. In a period of three weeks, I developed promotional materials, had a photo made, sent out a package, and scheduled a date by which I wanted to set sail. Before I had a chance to make a follow-up call to see if they were interested, they called me. I was booked to go on the cruise five months ahead of what I had scheduled and it was one of the easiest things I had ever done.

On the following pages, you will find forms you can use to develop the strategies and tactics you will need to create your own projects and make your dreams come true. Follow the simple "designing a blueprint" directions and walk through the process.

Designing a Blueprint

Here is a formula for getting into action on any project.

1. Outline or overview what's needed using the Strategies section.

> # If you want your
> # dreams to come true,
> # don't sleep.
> # —Yiddish proverb

2. Identify your Resources. Be creative.
3. Break the steps into single items to do in the Tactics section.
4. Add Dates and Resources.
5. Put in chronological order on the Scheduling page.
6. See where you are overscheduled and where you can *Reschedule*.
7. Be in *action* on your dream every day or at least every week.

Being Resourceful

A crucial component of creating successful strategies and tactics is making use of the resources in all the areas of your life. On pages 122–23, you will find forms you can use to write out who and what are your resources. Think about the people you know in the different aspects of your life; consider what's available to you in the way of technology and information. There's nothing that's not a potential resource. Your list may not be long, but it will be a way for you to leverage what you already have.

I'm an advocate of simplification and shortcuts. If you can find a faster way of getting something done, do it. One of your strategies might be to accomplish something that you don't know how to do, and one of your tactics might be to learn it.

STRATEGIES AND TACTICS:
A ROAD MAP FOR GETTING THERE

Strategies: Your Approach to Achieving Your Dream
and Completing Your Project

1. _____
2. _____
3. _____
4. _____
5. _____

Tactics: Your ``To Do'' List
(complete for each of the strategies you list above)

Date	Item	Resource
_____	_____	_____
_____	_____	_____
_____	_____	_____
_____	_____	_____
_____	_____	_____
_____	_____	_____
_____	_____	_____
_____	_____	_____
_____	_____	_____
_____	_____	_____
_____	_____	_____

Scheduling: Put the ''items to do'' in chronological order and transfer them to your calendar.

Month_____

Day_____ To do _____

_____ _____

_____ _____

_____ _____

_____ _____

Month_____

Day_____ To do _____

_____ _____

_____ _____

_____ _____

_____ _____

Month_____

Day_____ To do _____

_____ _____

_____ _____

_____ _____

_____ _____

Month_____

Day_____ To do _____

_____ _____

_____ _____

_____ _____

_____ _____

However, another tactic might be to hire or partner with somebody who already has that knowledge. By getting clear about your resources, you can cross-reference them with your dreams and projects, and determine how things might come together.

Strategies and tactics do go hand in hand, as illustrated in Brian's example at the end of this chapter. In developing a list of strategies and tactics, some people like to code them in a way that tells you at a glance what you have to do to accomplish them:

"S" means all you have to do is "schedule" them. Open your calendar and do so.

"B" means the strategy or tactic is a way for you to "be," rather than something you have to do. These are usually ongoing.

"P" means the strategy or tactic needs a "plan" to develop it further so that it can be scheduled into your calendar. Set up time to do this.

"D" is my favorite letter, because it means "done." It's wonderful when you can see what you've accomplished and that you're moving forward on your project.

When you get to this stage, it's important to differentiate between a project and a specific tactic. It's a lot easier to get into action on a tactic than it is on a whole project. You can accomplish your project one manageable tactic or one small step at a time.

The Dream Bank Deposit Slip

When you are looking for people who are committed to encouraging the possibilities in your life and to supporting your dreams, remember me. I'm one of those people. I believe that every aspect of all your dreams can come true, and I've created

MY RESOURCES

People and Organizations Who Can Help Me:
Friends who can help me: _____

_____

Friends of friends who can help me: _____

_____

Family members who can help me: _____

_____

Business associates who can help me: _____

_____

Organizations or associations that can help me: _____

_____

Who will support me? _____

_____

Who can advise me? _____

_____

Who can really help me? _____

_____

People I don't know who can help me: _____

_____

Who is the one person who won't help me? _____

_____

How can I use even the person who won't help? ____

_____

Things I Can Do to Make My Dream Come True:
Places I can go: _____

_____

Things I can read: _____

_____

New things I can try: _____

_____

Old things I can reference: _____

_____

The one place I know I can't get any help: _____

_____

How can I use this? _____

_____

The Dream Bank, where you can deposit how you want your life to be.

On pages 125–26, you will find Dream Bank Deposit Slips. I invite you to fill in all the information requested; then, where it says, "My dream is that by _____ I will do the following," take one of the tactics that make you want to get into action right away, and pick a date to accomplish it.

In fact, there are three duplicate deposit slips on the pages that follow. One can be used to pick a date a week from today. Write a specific task that you will complete this week. The task could be someone you're going to call, something you're going to write, something you're going to do, or research you're going to conduct. When you've completed next week's deposit slip, schedule the task by putting it on next week's calendar.

The second deposit slip is for something you will accomplish by the end of the year. Look at your projects, strategies, and tactics. What are you committed to making come true? When you have completed the end-of-the-year deposit slip, enter it at the top of this month's calendar and on the top of December's calendar. Design a real-time strategy to get you from tomorrow to the end of the year, and enter it, along with the tactics by which you will accomplish it, on your calendar.

Finally, use the last deposit slip to list a dream you will accomplish in this lifetime. Remember, this is your Bigger-Than-Life Dream that comes from your Purpose. It's about who you are and what excites you, about a way for you to accomplish something by which you want to be remembered. This final deposit slip will enable you to design passion into your life from this moment to the day you die. What can you do now to get into action on your "if" dream?

When you have completed all three deposit slips, photocopy the page, and send it to me at the address on the order form, page 205 at the back of the book. When I receive them, you'll become part of a global network, a Dreams Registry for people all over the world with all kinds of dreams.

If you choose not to send the copies to my Dreams Registry, fill in the deposit slips and tape them to your mirror, or put them in another place where you'll read them daily. It's powerful, however, to have your dreams registered with someone who believes they will come true. I'll be that person for you; I believe in you and in your having what you want.

I believe you will have your dreams come true.

REAL PEOPLE: BRIAN

Brian, the man who wanted to create a new foundation, decided that, to open for business, one of his strategies was to find office space. The tactics he chose were to look at a certain number of spaces by a specific date, to review his resources, to speak

DREAM BANK DEPOSIT SLIP #001

My dream is that by _____ I will do the following:
(date)

_____

_____

_____

_____

Name: _____

Address: _____

_____

Phone: (Home) _____ (Office) _____

DREAM BANK DEPOSIT SLIP #002

My dream is that by _____ I will do the following:
(date)

_____

_____

_____

_____

Name: _____

Address: _____

_____

Phone: (Home) _____ (Office) _____

Dream Bank Deposit Slip #003

My dream is that by _____ I will do the following:
(date)

_____

_____

_____

_____

Name: _____

Address: _____

_____

Phone: (Home) _____ (Office) _____

with other nonprofit organizations about sharing space, and to
be in new premises within a certain time frame. The most powerful tactic of all was that he committed himself to a specific date
and wrote it on his calendar.

There were many other strategies that Brian developed so that

> # Register your dreams
> # with someone who
> # believes that they
> # will come true.

he could open for business, including having the necessary office equipment, producing the marketing and promotional materials, setting up an accounting system, preparing a strategic plan for his board of directors, enlisting key people to support his vision, and raising funds.

Under the area of funding, Brian's tactics were to break down his operating income: by a certain date he would know what his expenses would be, and he would then identify thirty corporations and fifteen foundations that would each give him $25,000. To simplify his pursuit of funding, Brian broke down even those specifics into additional strategies and tactics. By breaking all his strategies down into specific items to do with due dates, Brian successfully accomplished his project and his dream.

It's a lot easier to get into action on a tactic than it is on a whole project.

PLAYING ON A
WINNING TEAM

A burning purpose attracts others who
are drawn along with it and help fulfill it.
—*Margaret Bourke-White*

Some people still harbor old beliefs that they have to do everything themselves. Perhaps it's that old John Wayne–type, individualistic, American frontier attitude. If you feel that standing on your own two feet means never accepting help from anyone, it's important to acknowledge the tendency. Of course, you *can* "go it alone" if you insist, but it's a longer, harder process.

I caution you, however, not to take on everything by yourself.

> You want to simplify
> the journey to
> having your dream,
> not complicate it.

If you're part of a winning team, you can accelerate progress, expand your horizons, and create additional opportunities—in short, it's easier and faster to do it with other people.

When I speak of a winning team, I don't necessarily mean a club or a group of people that meets with regularity. A formal group has potential for some people and not for others. Rather, I think of a winning team as a resource group, people to whom you can turn when you need advice, when you need a sounding board, when you need to cut through a thorny problem, or when you need someone to listen.

Although we all tend not to want to bother others or to recruit assistance, the Magic that happens whenever two or more are gathered is uncanny. I personally believe you're only a few phone calls away from anyone in the world that you need to contact. Use this to your advantage.

Letting others help you is a form of true generosity, because you enable them to feel good about contributing to your success. Many people love to make a difference by helping others. You can allow people to assist you most effectively by learning how to make powerful requests. Get clear about what you need, find the individuals who can help you get it, and ask for what you want.

One of the tools you can use to decide what skills you need on your team is to develop written criteria. On page 130, list your requirements for the members of your winning team.

Enrolling Others: Your Current Resources

Enrollment means sharing your dream with other people so that they get a sense of what's possible for themselves. It's not just about motivating people to help you; it's actually speaking your dream in such a way that other people begin to understand their potential to participate.

There are many reasons why others would be interested in participating with you. After all, you're a go-getter with a big dream; in its completion, your dream might benefit others. What happens out of enrollment is Magic, power, surprises, and results.

CRITERIA FOR MEMBERS OF YOUR WINNING TEAM

Skills: _____

_____

_____

Interests: _____

_____

_____

Education: _____

_____

_____

Resources: _____

_____

_____

Other: _____

_____

_____

For example, one of my dreams was to be out in the world speaking about something in which I believed. I shared my dream and connected, through a friend-of-a-friend, with someone who was director of creative services for a national television network. The network person eventually scheduled me on a nationwide talk show, something that might not have happened if I had not been speaking about my dream.

With whom should you speak? Begin by reviewing the Resources forms completed in chapter 11, to see who's available in your current world to help. Start talking to those people about your dream. Tell them what it is you're committed to; help them to experience your excitement by sharing your enthusiasm with them.

Ask your resources whom else they know. Remember, you're only one phone call away from somebody you need to reach, two at the most. By asking those you know to name others, you are developing a network. Before long, you will have clarified your needs and you'll start to understand whom you want on your team. Some people feel they may disempower their dreams by sharing them with too many people. I believe that by speaking powerfully to your resources and the people you have taught to hear and support your dreams, you will enhance and empower yourself greatly.

You know some people right now who can fill spots on your team immediately, and you'll find others during the process. If you need a confidant, someone to whom you can tell all your secrets, look around among your resources; that person may already exist. If someone with business savvy does not exist among your current resources, find out if anyone you know is acquainted with such a person; if not, go out and find the individuals with the skills you need.

Enrolling Others: New Resources

Your team need not be composed only of people who are currently on your Resource list. When you need additional skills on the team, add new members who are outside of your immediate universe.

You can find new people with the skills you need by identify-

*The people you need
to help you make your
dream come true are
everywhere, and
within your reach.*

ing groups and associations to which they may belong. Several directories list organizations by subject area: for example, *Gale's Encyclopedia of Associations* or the *National Trade and Professional Associations of the United States.* Ask people you already know what associations they belong to; look in the business section of your local newspaper to identify groups that meet in your area.

Plan to attend group meetings as a nonmember, go with your Purpose in mind, and be clear about the intended result. Decide in advance what kind of people you want to meet there, what you want to get out of the meeting, and what you want to communicate. Once you're there, you have an opportunity to develop relationships with all kinds of new people; plan to participate and interact with them. Always speak your dream powerfully.

If you notice that someone is getting excited about your dream, ask how that individual would like to participate. You start with a blank slate among new people; capture the energy and input from those encounters.

It is also powerful to ask others about their commitment to their own dream. As they speak, you might discover a way to join with them and further your vision. For instance, someone who's committed to literacy might be able to help you fulfill

> *Many ideas grow better when transplanted into another mind, than in the one where they sprang up.*
> *—Justice Oliver Wendell Holmes*

your dream of creating more jobs for people. Perhaps together you can find employment for previously unemployable people who have learned how to read. By listening to other people's dreams, you can open up the possibilities and let the Magic appear in your own.

Another way to enroll people onto your winning team is to become an active letter writer. Whenever someone who can further your dream is mentioned in a book or an article, or is featured on radio or television, note how to contact the publication or the station. Take a risk; write a letter, and tell that individual about your dream.

Perhaps you will be attending a convention featuring a speaker you'd like to have as part of your network. Write in advance and say how much you look forward to the presentation. While you're at the meeting, approach that person and introduce yourself; then write a quick follow-up letter when the meeting is over. These simple steps will take you less than an hour. By doing them, you will have made yourself part of that new person's consciousness and, in the months that follow, you can begin a professional dialogue.

Don't be afraid to call people on the phone. If you're not sure exactly what you want to say, write out a couple of points and keep them in front of you, or practice speaking to some-body else.

Jeff Davidson, in his popular book *Blow Your Own Horn: How to Get Noticed—And Get Ahead,* suggests that you think about the ten people you need to call right now. Perhaps they include an association director, a magazine editor, or someone in another industry. You will find the task less formidable if you break it down into its individual components. First, compile a list of the phone numbers and have them in front of you. Then commit to making a specific number of calls each day. Get into action.

> Look for resources in your own company.
> With whom can you speak about your dream when you go to work tomorrow morning?
> Is your boss enrolled, or any of your co-workers?
> Do they even know that you have a dream?

Are you keeping your dream a secret, tucked under your pil-low? Have you already decided that they're not potential part-ners and they can't help you? Or are you sitting there thinking that you can't pursue your dream without your boss's support, even though your boss may not know what your dream is? Don't kill off possibilities before you've explored them.

Look for ways to share your dream and tie it into the other aspects of your life. It's essential that you enroll your family in your dream by communicating what you want. Let them hear your commitment and enthusiasm, and be unstoppable regard-less of how they respond. As they see your commitment, no matter how big the dream may be, eventually they will stand behind you.

Show them you're not giving up; ask them to support you, even if it's only by believing in you, and be open to receiving their support.

Sometimes we feel absolutely sure that we cannot get the support we want from the people from whom we want it most.

WHO ARE THE TEN PEOPLE
YOU KNOW YOU NEED TO CALL?

1. _____

2. _____

3. _____

4. _____

5. _____

6. _____

7. _____

8. _____

9. _____

10. _____

TENACITY OFTEN YIELDS CREDIBILITY.

Let them change their minds. Any day, any minute, could be the moment they sign up to be on your team.

When you think about involving your family, notice your attitudes and beliefs. Is that voice inside your head saying "My parents never thought I could do it" or "The family will think I'm off on another harebrained scheme"? Those are just your attitudes and beliefs; you can go back and write them in the attitudes and beliefs section in chapter 6, but you don't have to include them in what you are designing for the future.

Be clear about what you're committed to, and speak it clearly so that people around you can help. Get others on board, whether they play an intimate role in your dream or a tangential one. It's all part of building a winning team.

The Members of Your Winning Team

Whenever you enroll others, one of the ways to engage them quickly is to make a request. Ask for something specific; the more precise the request, the more specific the response. Simply say, "I'd like to make a request of you." Your query can be accepted or declined, or the other person can make a counteroffer. When you make a request, be willing to hear what people say in response.

When you ask for something, you signal to others that your

interest in what they have to offer is more than casual. You convey the message that you'd like to have an answer, that you're interested in moving the conversation and, possibly, the relationship forward.

Once you've got someone's attention, you can enlist their services in several ways. One of my favorite methods is to trade services. One woman I know conducts public relations activities for her certified public accountant in exchange for accounting assistance. Someone else trades strategic planning services for massage therapy.

If you think you don't have anything to barter, reexamine what you're passionate about. Everyone can offer some kind of service they can exchange for another. It's a great way of experiencing what you're capable of doing.

The Skills on Your Team

There are many kinds of skills you will need on your winning team, although you can expect your needs to change over time. As you develop new projects and complete old ones, you may find yourself in need of talents you did not consider important earlier. However, there are three kinds of people you will always need on your team: mentors, coaches, and partners. List your candidates on page 138.

Mentors. People who "know the ropes" are an invaluable asset. The skills required of a mentor are perhaps the easiest to define, and the easiest to find. If you are looking for someone who can teach you how to move forward quickly, or how to create shortcuts, or how to break into a new area you're interested in, you need only seek someone with expertise in the field.

A lawyer, for example, can mentor another; a woman who runs her own business can guide an entrepreneur who is starting out; an experienced writer can assist a fledgling author. Look for someone who has been where you want to go, is still learning and growing, and is happy to share those experiences with you.

Mentors:

Coaches:

Partners:

Coaches. A coach is someone who listens for what's possible, helps you break through when you're stuck, and holds you accountable for doing what you said you were going to do.

Coaches are not usually listed in the Yellow Pages, but there are lots of trained professionals available for hire. You can employ a strategic planner or a marketing specialist; or you can train a close friend to take your dreams seriously and see their possibilities.

Look for someone with qualities you admire: strength of character, clarity of vision, commitment, dependability. Once you identify your coach, design the coaching relationship using some or all of the questions on page 140.

Partners. Partners are people who will give, receive, and share equally with you as members of your winning team. You can develop partnerships with individuals who are already in your life—family members, friends, business associates—or with organizations and groups of individuals.

When you know what result you want from a partner on your team, allow other possibilities to open up. Sometimes simply picking up the phone and having a conversation of possibility with someone might initiate something new. A project is the glue that will allow you and your partner to work together. Design a venture you're both clear about, with specific, measurable results; out of that, the partnership will develop.

As you review the list of resources, you might notice that there are dozens of people in your life of whom you never thought to make a request, or unique combinations of individuals whom you never before thought of putting together.

You won't want to feel overwhelmed, however, about where you'll find the time for new ventures. If you're creating your winning team on track, everything you do will support your Purpose, support your dreams, and be filled with passion. That's always your touchstone for making sure that you're on target toward making your dream come true.

In what area do you want to be coached?

What is the specific, measurable result that you want?

What is your weekly campaign of activities?

How often will you and your coach speak?

For what length of time?

How do you want to be coached?

Do you want to know when you're doing it right and wrong?

Are you going to be open to hearing criticism as ``coaching,'' or will you hear it as judgment?

THE GOOSE STORY

Next fall, when you see geese heading south for the winter
. . . flying along in V formation . . . consider what science has
discovered as to why they fly that way.

As each bird flaps its wings, it creates
an uplift for the bird immediately following.

By flying in V formation, the whole flock adds at least 71
percent greater flying range than if each bird flew on its own.

People who share a common direction and sense of community
can get where they are going more quickly and easily
because they are traveling on the thrust of one another.

When a goose falls out of formation, it suddenly feels the drag
and resistance of trying to go it alone . . . and quickly gets back into
formation to take advantage of the lifting power of the bird in front.

If we have as much sense as a goose we will stay in
formation with those who are headed the same way we are.

When the Head Goose gets tired, it rotates back
in the wing and another goose flies the point.

It is sensible to take turns doing demanding jobs
with people or with geese flying south.

Geese honk from behind to encourage those up
front to keep up their speed.

What do we say when we honk from behind?

Finally,
and this is important,
when a goose gets sick or is wounded by gunshots and
falls out of formation, two other geese fall out with that goose
and follow it down to lend help and protection.

They stay with the fallen goose until it is able to fly,
or until it dies; and only then do they launch out on their own,
or with another formation to catch up with their group.

If we have the sense of a goose,
We will stand by each other like that.

—Source unknown

COMMUNICATING YOUR DREAM AS A WAY OF LIVING

The difference between the right word and the almost right word is the difference between lightning and the lightning bug.
—Mark Twain

You have assembled a winning team, and you've become adept at enrolling more and more people who are interested in what you're doing. To accelerate toward your dream, you will want to continue communicating effectively with your team, and with others as well.

The members of your team need to hear you speak your dream, or they won't know how they can help you. You might feel a little awkward at first, but the more you articulate your dream, the more powerful you'll become. Like anything else, it requires practice.

In today's world, people are inundated by enormous amounts of information competing for their attention. For example, in 1968, the portion of a statement or speech used for television news, called a "soundbite," ran an average of 42 seconds. By 1988, soundbites were down to 9.8 seconds.

In other words, you have less than ten seconds to speak your dream; that's about how much time you have for someone to understand what you're trying to do. If you want to break through the information din, practice saying what you want to

COMMUNICATING YOUR DREAM

In twenty-five words or less, write in the space below a clear description of your dream or your project.

_____

_____

_____

_____

Now rate yourself on the Passion Scale. If you're not excited about your dream, others won't be either. Listen to yourself; hear how you sound. See how you feel. Tell us about your dream.

PASSION SCALE

Place an X next to the area that best describes your level of passion regarding speaking about your dream or project. Do it right now.

_____Red-hot

_____Turned on

_____Excited

_____Very interested

_____Interested

_____Some possibility

_____No interest

say, and see if you can get it across clearly and comfortably in ten seconds.

The ten-second exercise may surprise you. In fact, you can complete three sentences within that amount of time. For example, the words you are reading in this paragraph can be said in about ten seconds.

On page 144 there is space to write your dream or your project in twenty-five words or less. Write it, practice speaking it aloud, then practice by speaking it to other people. If others don't understand your message immediately, revise it until they do. Here are some examples of brief, distinct descriptions:

- I intend to speak with one hundred people about rain forest preservation, and to create a television series about it.
- I'm going to hold a one-day seminar for children of divorced parents.
- I will make available to all employees at my company an effective program for retirement savings.
- I plan to invent the best relationship with a man that I can have.

The expression of what you want can be simple or it can be sophisticated. Base your decision on the nature of the dream you're committed to creating. Mine is to have people speak about dreams in a new way, to believe that dreams are something they can have come true in their lifetime. What's yours?

Who's Listening?

When you tell people what your dream is, you will want to know whether they've heard you. Look into their eyes; are they confused or upset about what you're saying? Are they excited and "with you"? Do they understand? If you're not sure, stop and find out. Ask them what they think. If they're not excited about your dream, it doesn't mean that you did something wrong; it

> An orator is a man
> who says what he thinks
> and feels what he says.
> —William Jennings Bryan

may not be the right dream for them. They can still be your friends or business associates, but not people you want on your winning team.

Remember that when *you* started to go for your dream, you had a variety of negative attitudes, beliefs, concerns, and fears; others might also harbor attitudes that are limiting. People who care about you may feel especially convinced that you're going in the wrong direction, taking too much risk, or putting yourself in an unstable situation by breaking out of the norm.

Train people to listen to you. Explain what the word ''possibility'' means, and ask them to hear what's possible for *you*.

> *Notice who's listening*
> *to you and how they're*
> *listening, and train them*
> *to hear what you're saying*
> *in a way that's powerful.*

Request that they suspend their automatic negative reactions and judgments, and that they hear your dream from your perspective.

You don't necessarily have to convince people to see things your way to receive their support. It may take them a while before they're comfortable about accepting your dream. In the meantime, commit yourself to the possibility of getting their support in exactly the way you've asked for it. Believe that you can have that kind of relationship, and keep speaking your dream.

If you think it will overwhelm people, you may not want to speak all of your dream in one sitting. You can do it in stages; keep living and speaking what you want, and sharing it with others so they can experience what's going on for you. Eventually, they will reach the stage at which, whether times are good or bad, you can share your dream completely.

Maybe everyone won't reach such a stage. At some point, you may decide that a particular person won't fit on your winning team. That happens sometimes, and it's good to know when you have enough information to make that decision. However, I encourage you not to write people off at the beginning if they don't align with your dream. Request that they consider what you are saying, and give them a chance to do so.

When you share your dream, it's okay also to speak about your fears and concerns. If others are facing the same fears and concerns, the issues can be put on the table for discussion. You may recall that, in chapter 6, we spoke of the importance of honesty about your current reality; sharing that truth with another person can be an insightful experience.

Part of the communications process involves dancing the dance of interaction. Trust, let the conversation flow, and listen to what is being said. Something new might show up: perhaps they know of a new resource; maybe they will suggest a new way for you to look at something. Don't be rigidly attached to what is already in your mind. In speaking your dream, new opportunities will show up, and Magic will occur.

The story of Gillian appears below and illustrates the benefits of enrolling others. What's important about Gillian's story is that a major international event started with somebody's dream. The vision became bigger and took on new form when Gillian began speaking her dream and enrolling others. All kinds of opportunities showed up, and different people became part of the winning team to make it a success.

This is an example of how a dream became a reality; how communication and sharing got people enrolled and excited; and how the dream became bigger and better than what any individual at first thought was possible.

REAL PEOPLE: GILLIAN

Gillian was the head of the U.S. contingent of the World Association of Women Entrepreneurs. Her dream was to invite women from all over the world to Washington, D.C., where they would be treated in a special way.

Gillian spoke her dream to Virginia, who became excited about it. Together, Gillian and Virginia organized a group of women to brainstorm around Gillian's idea. The result was a decision to conduct a major luncheon and media event in the nation's capital.

The objective of the luncheon was to honor women entrepreneurs from various countries around the world, and to have them recognized by other women business owners, by government officials, and by the media. The exposure and visibility was expected to garner greater national attention for the organization, additional funds, an increase in U.S. membership, and a boost to the organization's international membership.

As the brainstorming continued, the women decided to create "The Declaration of International Partnership." They developed

> When you begin speaking your
> dream and enrolling others,
> your dream can get bigger
> and take on new forms,
> and all kinds of
> opportunities will show up.

a document that focused on five areas in which women business owners could make an impact: education, environment, enterprise, communication, and innovation.

Some five hundred people attended the event, which was held at the National Press Club. Women representing twenty-eight countries signed the document. The luncheon was hailed as an historic event, and got major TV and print exposure, including the international edition of *USA Today*.

Every dream starts with an idea and grows proportionately to the amount of energy, excitement, and commitment behind it.

WOMEN ENTREPRENEURS OF WORLD GATHER IN D.C.

Women make up over half of the world's population, contribute two-thirds of the world's working hours, receive one-tenth of the world's income and own only 1/100ths of the world's property.

But by the year 2000, more than half of all businesses will be owned by women.

Wednesday, women business owners from 22 countries gathered in Washington, D.C. for the first-ever meeting in the USA of the group, Les Femmes Chefs D'Entreprises Mondiales—or Women Entrepreneurs of the World.

''We want to promote more trade, provide cross-cultural training and support, set up programs to educate women, and provide scholarships,'' says Marcia Wieder, president of the Washington chapter of the USA's National Association of Women Business Owners.

The women—from countries including France, Italy, Austria, Spain, Taiwan, India and Cameroon—will tour the World Bank, the White House and the Capitol and other sites as part of a four-day tour of Washington. First on the agenda: a signing ceremony to announce the ''Declaration of International Partnership.''

Maria Grazia Gatti Randi, 65, president of a public relations firm in Milan, Italy, will preside. She is president of the international women's group.

—*Mindy Fetterman*

First appeared in *USA Today.*

CHAPTER FOURTEEN

DESIGNING YOUR ENVIRONMENT

*Two stonecutters were asked what they were doing. The first
said, "I'm cutting this stone into blocks." The second replied,
"I'm on a team that's building a cathedral."*
—An old story

Enrolling others to support your dream is one important aspect
of using resources. Another is designing your environment. As
you progress on the path to making your dream come true, and
you begin to realize that more and more is possible, additional
opportunities and resources begin to become available. Whereas
you may once have been concerned about not having any possibilities, now you may feel overwhelmed by them.

The process is dynamic and ongoing. As you enroll people in
your dream, you generate additional projects. As you take on
other projects and develop new resources, you discover other
people you wish to enroll. The new people lead you to new
projects, and you find yourself constantly rearranging your
physical and emotional environment to support your new en-
deavors.

The point of designing your environment is to create an atmo-
sphere that will accommodate your changing needs while remaining clutter-free. You began the process way back in chapter
1 when you first started looking at your passion. That is, after
all, the environment for which you are designing. Aligning your
dreams with your Purpose—removing the inconsistencies—
was just another way of removing clutter.

> *As you progress on the path to making your dream come true, you begin to realize that more and more is possible.*

You might start this phase of designing your environment with something as simple as cleaning off your desk or organizing your closet. There are many books written about eliminating physical clutter; don't belabor it, do it so you will have space to continue creating and reaching for your dream. Similarly, if there are emotional issues keeping you from being clear about what your dream will look like, or about how you'll have the time to get it, clear them out of your way.

Finding Time

Time is a funny thing. Sometimes we feel that it's closing in around us; but when there's something we're passionate about, we create the time to make it happen.

Each of my project files has a list of strategies and tactics—the items to do—attached to the front of it. If I'm in my office with an extra hour between calls, I can pull out one of my project files, do any item on the list, and I'm in action on something I love in my life. I spend all my time working on my projects. At the end of the day or the week, when I want to plan ahead, I look at my project files and create the next week.

Projects are the mechanism for fulfilling your Life's Purpose.

It takes focus and commitment to design your whole life to work this way. It takes time, too, to learn a completely new way to live, think, and plan. Keep it simple at first, so you won't feel overwhelmed. Perhaps there's one area of your life in which you can start to live on purpose, one dream that matters to you, one project that will ignite the passion in you. Maybe it's not a project that exists yet. Maybe it's something you're going to create that comes from your heart. If you schedule it, I promise that you'll have the time to do it.

Even if you are employed by a company where most of the projects you work on have been assigned, you can still find one area where you're in control, then slowly begin to work on other areas. Maybe there's a project you can bring into your company; or a project that already exists to which you're not now assigned, but which is in alignment with your interests. If you're not passionate at work, think about what you can bring to the job that will allow you to bring passion there. Maybe there's a piece of something you feel passionate about that you can integrate into a work project. If you can't invest your job with passion, perhaps you are turned on by an issue in your community. Follow your passion. Pursue what has heart and meaning for you.

Simplify

If you have so many things going in your life that you need to clear some out before you can get to higher ground, there's something you can do about that: simplify. Here's how.

Go back to your Purpose, the simple, broad terms of who you are, and revisit your dreams. Cross-reference that massive list of "to do's," projects, and all the other things you've got going on, and see how they align with your dreams. Perhaps amid all that clutter, there's actually something missing, an area left out of your dreams, such as having a balanced life.

Now you have another choice to make. You can add another dream, or you can take a critical look at your projects to see if you're committed to all of them. Perhaps they're not all on your "A" list. If you're compulsive about not giving anything up, and you decide that you're committed to everything, maybe there's something you don't absolutely have to do this year. Or you may decide that it's fine to eliminate the four or five projects you feel burdened by, the ones that aren't even listed under a dream you think is important.

You can ease up in your desire to have something, your com-

> There is always a way
> to create a life that
> supports who you are,
> and there are always
> places where things
> can be relaxed.

mitment to it, your schedule, or in the degree to which you need to have it. It all starts with that foundation called your Life's Purpose, the "Who are you, really?" and "Just what are you committed to?"

There are other ways to design your environment besides clearing out the clutter and finding time. I like to create blueprints, mechanisms for getting from point A to point B. In the Real People story at the end of this chapter, you will see that creating a blueprint is what we did for David, using imagery that will keep his commitment always in front of him.

Perhaps all you need to begin designing your own environment is to cut out photos from a magazine and hang them in a prominent place, as mentioned earlier. Maybe, like David, there's something you can develop as part of your physical self so that you can stay easily in touch with your dream and always keep it right in front of you.

Shortcuts and the Myth of Prerequisites

With his five professional areas of interest mapped out in front of him, David started looking for shortcuts to his dream, and for short-circuits in his beliefs. His search for short-circuits was appropriate; that small voice in his head was admonishing him that he "had to do A before he could do B."

Tie things together
to simplify the journey
on the road
to your dream.

Everyone has such internal dialogues: "I'll do it when I have the money, when I get the education, when my family's ready to support me, after my children are grown." Somebody once told me that she always wanted to be a doctor, but she never could amass the time or money to go to medical school.

When she got in touch with what made her feel passionate, she saw that she wanted to work in the medical field, but she didn't want to be a doctor. When she was relieved of the burdens of facing how she would go through medical school, she quickly arranged for the training she needed to become an emergency medical technician.

Sometimes people become paralyzed by the belief that, to move on, they need certain skills or additional assets. Yet there are often resources readily available to help them move quickly through the process of getting their dream. One method, of course, is skill building; another is finding or hiring somebody who has the skills to do it for you. The advice of mentors, coaches, and partners, which we discussed in chapter 12, is another great way to find a shortcut.

In addition to external resources, you have, in yourself, a major resource. You can move yourself forward by being clear about what you want to do, by deciding whether your goals in one area support those in another, and by tying things together to simplify the journey on the road to your dream.

If you're giving a speech, for example, and you videotape it, you can use the tape to make other programs and to send to speakers' bureaus and radio stations. You are in the best position to design your environment in ways to make your life easier. Make them up, try them on, tie them together.

Make requests of other people that are beyond what you thought was initially possible. Get up an hour earlier or an hour later. Flip through magazines you don't normally read. Find new ways to see things by trying on someone else's glasses, closing your eyes and finding a new perspective, going to a

> *One of your most*
> *powerful inner resources*
> *is your own creativity.*
> *Be willing to try on*
> *something new and*
> *play the game full-out.*

children's movie or a play, relaxing, using your intuition. There are many methods of breaking out of your box; you only need to look for them.

For example, there are a variety of ways to look at your current life and the resources that you already have available. We discussed some of them in chapter 11, but have you considered all the places that you frequent in the course of a week?

Your office
Your health club
Your doctor's office
The supermarket
Movie theaters
Restaurants

Perhaps there are resources among the people who supply you with goods or services. Maybe there's something you can tap into at your alma mater, through special courses and seminars you've attended, or teachers you've had. Think about all the cities in all the countries where you know people, or have met people in the past.

Everything in your life is a possibility, especially yourself.

Examine how *you* look and speak as a resource, not just with whom you are speaking. Are you friendly and open? Do you have high powers of concentration? Do you go out dancing, to concerts, plays, or shows? Are you willing to let people help you? Do you?

What about the books you read, the videos you watch, the ideas you have, the energy you give off, even when you're dreaming in your sleep at night? Everything that you experience is a resource you can use to design your environment. Write down possible resources on page 159. How are you using your resources?

Freedom—Letting Go

Many of us have a very basic dream that has to do with freedom.

I'd love to have the freedom to do whatever I want whenever I want.

Or the freedom to travel anywhere and everywhere.

Or, my favorite, the freedom to shop without looking at price tags.

However, many of us are stuck with that old belief about prerequisites—the idea that we have to do something or have something in order to be free. For a long time, I wanted to move to California. I decided I'd move as soon as I could sell my Washington, D.C., condominium. Months went by, and it didn't sell. I knew that the apartment wasn't selling for a reason, that there was something for me to learn in this. I've learned to be suspicious about prerequisites, and asked myself, "What's really keeping me from moving now?" The answer was fear. I was afraid of the unknown, of giving up everything I knew. But that was just part of my current reality. Even with this fear, I was clearly committed to my dream to live in California.

One day, I pulled out my journal and asked myself, "What will I do or be in California that I'm not doing or being here and now in Washington, D.C.?" What a splendid question.

On my "doing" list, I wrote, "Playing tennis, 'doing lunch,'

RESOURCES I HADN'T PREVIOUSLY CONSIDERED

_____

_____

_____

_____

_____

_____

_____

_____

_____

_____

_____

_____

_____

_____

_____

> # You don't have to go somewhere in order to be free; you can be free anywhere.

growing my hair long, not working every day, public speaking." On my "being" list, I wrote, "Playing, meditating, beaching, listening, waking without an alarm clock, breathing, believing, and being near the water."

I began to do and be everything on my lists while I was still in D.C., and everything magically became possible. That brought me to a major revelation: I could be free anywhere. I didn't have to go somewhere or do something in order to be free.

Once I had that realization, it was easy to let go of an old belief that was keeping me from the freedom I wanted, and I sold the condo. As a matter of fact, I committed to moving West before the sale, and then the sale happened.

Money Madness

Probably the most overworked excuse for not having what we want, or for not pursuing our dreams, is money—"If I only had [pick a number from $100 to $1 million], then I'd go for my dream." My response to this is to do it anyway. Find a way to be in action. Develop alternatives. Get creative.

Find or devise the means to start now. If I hadn't sold my condo, I would have rented it. As Joseph Kennedy, Sr., said, "When the going gets tough, the tough get going."

Are you holding on to the very thing you want to be free of?

Find yourself a different perspective. Trust me—money doesn't need to ever, ever be the obstacle that keeps you from your dream.

Figure out what your belief about money is, and what your attitude is about money and your dreams. Find another "way in." Use money as a motivator or as a stepping stone, as a bridge from where you are to where you want to be.

If you hear yourself using money as an excuse, don't you believe it. There's something else going on. Check your core beliefs, change your core beliefs using the information in chapter 7, and do what you love. The money will follow.

Of course, money *is* one way to gain freedom, but it's not the only way. Martin Luther King, Jr., once said he could be locked in prison and he would still be free, because freedom lived in his heart. Now, that's freedom!

What prerequisites have you put in your own way that slow you down or keep you from having your dream?

REAL PEOPLE: DAVID

David is a television and film director who wanted to do some quick "blueprinting" of the design for his life. We were having dinner at a restaurant in Los Angeles. The restaurant used paper tablecloths and made crayons available for patrons to amuse

> *You are surrounded by resources to support you in making your dream come true.*

themselves while they waited for their food. David and I got into a conversation about what made him feel passionate, then we picked up some crayons and started to design David's environment. It was evident that David's Purpose was to be creative.

He said that he was turned on by five areas of his professional life: producing, directing, editing, acting, and writing. We brainstormed to find a symbol that he could always keep with him to remind him of his five passionate dream areas. We decided to use the fingers on a hand. So we traced David's hand on the paper, wrote his name in his palm, and each one of his fingers became one of his five passions.

Coming from his Purpose, David established one dream in each area that he was committed to accomplishing. Then he created three or four projects in every area, each project having specific, measurable results. David was turned on by the process, and the whole year was extraordinary for him; everything he did professionally fit into one of those five areas. Prior to doing the exercise, David felt he wasn't moving forward on his dream. Now he had designed and organized it in a way that made him feel powerful and get into action. Moreover, using his hand as a representation enabled David to reinforce with ease his dream and his commitment to it.

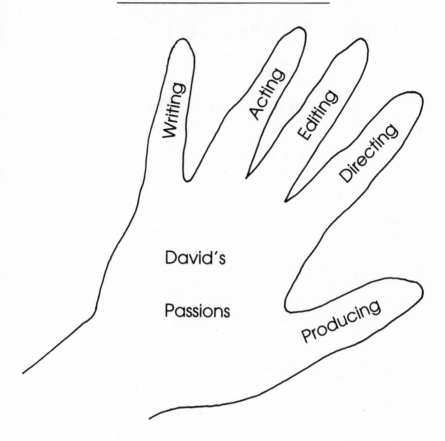

Writing

Acting

Editing

Directing

David's

Passions

Producing

PREPARING YOUR OWN DREAMS COME TRUE WORKBOOK

*The future belongs to those who believe
in the beauty of their dreams.*
—Eleanor Roosevelt

Over the years, one of the most effective vehicles I've found to ensure getting what you want is to prepare your own Making Your Dreams Come True Workbook. There is a sample Workbook at the end of this chapter, which I have left blank so you can use it to start your own.

Don't worry about having enough time to develop your Workbook; if you've progressed this far in the volume, you've done a lot of the work already. Now it's a matter of setting it up in a way that will allow you to live in your dream.

You don't have to do original work here; you can go back and copy the information you need from the Passion Pyramid or any of the notes you might have made while working through earlier chapters. Begin by filling in your Life's Purpose. Then, write the dream you're committed to accomplishing, and list the projects you've designed to fulfill that dream.

You will remember that, to simplify things, you chose one area on which to focus while going through this book. Now you have an opportunity to go back to all your dreams and list four or five different projects for each dream, with specific, measurable results.

Your Dreams Come True Workbook
will help you to set things up
in a way that will allow you
to live your dream.

You can list next to each project what the strategies and tactics are to accomplish them.

If you have a lot of projects, you can break them down even further. Thus, your completed Dreams Come True Workbook will consist of one overview sheet with your Purpose and dreams, a page for each of your dreams and its projects, and individual project sheets, listing all your strategies and tactics.

When you have completed that part of your Workbook, go back through your strategies and tactics and start to make notes in the margin about resources that are available to you. Maybe there's a project you're not clear about, one you can't exactly envision. Look for inspiration to clarify it. Perhaps you can see three movies in the next month that will spur creative ideas about how to accomplish that project. Even if you can't see it clearly yet, looking for inspiration is one way to be in action on a project that supports your Purpose and your dream.

Your Dreams Come True Workbook can be designed into a simple three-ring binder, broken down into the various sections: the overview, your Purpose, your dreams, your projects. However, don't be rigid about your Workbook; you may want to change its format as you go along. In any event, give yourself lots of room to expand. You will find that your initial projects turn into other projects—often more creative, challenging, and rewarding—and one opportunity will lead to another. You won't know at first all the avenues that will become open to you; that's part of the Magic.

It's essential that you keep using any tool that you develop for getting what you want. That's why your Dreams Come True Workbook needs to be tied to your calendar, whether you put a calendar in your Workbook or use your Workbook side by side with your existing appointment book. Keep your Workbook someplace visible and easily accessible. Open it every day. It's a way for you to reread your dream, and reconnect to your commitment. The power in doing so is that your

Since the mind is a specific
biocomputer, it needs specific
instructions and directions.
The reason most people never reach
their goals is that they don't define them,
learn about them, or ever seriously consider
them as believable or achievable.
Winners can tell you where they are
going, what they plan to do along the way,
and who will be sharing the
adventure with them.
—Dennis Waitley

> *Your Dreams Come True Workbook is a way for you to reread your dream, and reconnect to your commitment.*

dream exists outside of your head as well as in it; what you want is all there, with lots of clarity, right in front of you.

Use your Workbook also as a place for you to hold your resources. Buy the plastic sleeves available in office supply stores so that you can store news clippings or other flimsy materials. Establish sections in your Workbook for dreams you haven't yet fully developed. For example, if you want to move from being a teacher into doing lectures, create a section called "Lectures." If you want to initiate more bartering relationships, develop a "Bartering" section. You'll be surprised at how quickly you'll start to fill in those pages.

In the financial area of my own Workbook, I have sections for all the different ways that are available for me to make money: brokering, consulting, speaking, training, book sales, other products and services, investments, promotions, sponsorship opportunities. Your Workbook, in the area of personal finances, might include insurance plans, stock investments, trust funds, retirement accounts, certificates of deposit, stocks and bonds, educational funds, contributions, and so forth. In any aspect of your life for which you have a project, look for ways to subdivide the components; when you do, you will find more areas of opportunity that support and reinforce you in reaching your dream.

Remember that the power of your Workbook is that you have a place to hold your dreams. Don't be concerned that you don't know how you're going to accomplish all the different things you're committed to having; simply create the space and allow some of the Magic to show up.

MAKING YOUR DREAMS COME TRUE WORKBOOK

_____

Your Name

What is your dream or the essence of your dream?

_____

_____

_____

_____

_____

What do you intend to accomplish or create with this book?

_____

_____

_____

_____

_____

List three memories of passion or accomplishments:

1._____
_____
_____

2._____
_____
_____

3._____
_____
_____

My Life's Purpose is:

#1

_____
_____
_____
_____
_____

#2—Memorable ``soundbite''

_____
_____
_____

Dream Areas to Explore

If my Life's Purpose is _____
my dream is to:

Personal _____

_____

Professional _____

_____

Relationships _____

_____

Well-being _____

_____

Financial _____

_____

Fun _____

_____

Other or outrageous _____

_____

_____

Checkpoints

Does each one ``come from'' your
Purpose?   __Yes __No
Does it line up?   __Yes __No
Does this dream turn you on?   __Yes __No
Are you passionate about the
possibility this presents?   __Yes __No
   If you answered ``No,'' change the dream.

Life Area (Personal, Professional, Fun, etc.):

_____

Dream:

_____

_____

Projects   **Key**

1. _____ ___

_____ ___

2. _____ ___

_____ ___

3. _____ ___

_____ ___

4. _____ ___

_____ ___

5. _____ ___

_____ ___

Key
B - Being
S - Schedule
P - Plan
D - Done

My Dream, Assuming Unlimited Resources

Describe your dream: _____

_____

What are you doing? _____

_____

Where are you doing it? _____

_____

How do you feel? _____

_____

How do you look? _____

_____

Who are you with? _____

_____

What does your day look like? _____

_____

What are you creating or accomplishing? _____

_____

Give some detail: _____

_____

Give more detail: _____

_____

Attitudes & Beliefs

Your core beliefs create your thoughts and feelings, which either empower or impede your choices and decisions. As they surface, either mentally or verbally, write your core beliefs here.

Attitudes & Beliefs
< create >
Thoughts & Feelings
< which create >
Choices & Decisions

My limiting beliefs include: _____

_____

_____

_____

My empowering beliefs include: _____

_____

_____

_____

Changing Your Belief

My limiting belief that is stopping me from having my dream come true is:

_____

_____

_____

_____

_____

My wonderful new belief is:

_____

_____

_____

_____

_____

My Dream—Version 2

Now what's possible?_____

_____

_____

_____

Are you committed to having this dream
come true?
Yes____ No____

Do you believe it's possible?
Yes____ No____

If you answered ''Yes,'' go on; if you answered
''No,'' go back to the ''Changing Your Belief''
section.

From Dream to Project
or
From Dream to Reality

What project can you CREATE that represents, or will get you going on, your dream?
Criterion: A project needs to be specific, measurable, and have a completion date.
Hint: You may simply add a "by when" date to your dream from the previous page.

Project: By _____ (date)

_____

_____

_____

_____

_____

Strategies and Tactics:
A Road Map for Getting There

Strategies:
1. _____
2. _____
3. _____
4. _____
5. _____
6. _____

For Strategy #__, the tactics (items to do) are:

Date_____   Item_____   Resource_____
Date_____   Item_____   Resource_____
Date_____   Item_____   Resource_____
Date_____   Item_____   Resource_____
Date_____   Item_____   Resource_____
Date_____   Item_____   Resource_____
Date_____   Item_____   Resource_____
Date_____   Item_____   Resource_____
Date_____   Item_____   Resource_____
Date_____   Item_____   Resource_____
Date_____   Item_____   Resource_____
Date_____   Item_____   Resource_____
Date_____   Item_____   Resource_____
Date_____   Item_____   Resource_____
Date_____   Item_____   Resource_____
Date_____   Item_____   Resource_____
Date_____   Item_____   Resource_____
Date_____   Item_____   Resource_____
Date_____   Item_____   Resource_____
Date_____   Item_____   Resource_____
Date_____   Item_____   Resource_____
Date_____   Item_____   Resource_____
Date_____   Item_____   Resource_____
Date_____   Item_____   Resource_____
Date_____   Item_____   Resource_____

Resources: Things I Can Do
to Help Make My Dream Come True

Places I can go: _____

_____

_____

_____

Things I can read: _____

_____

_____

_____

New things I can try: _____

_____

_____

_____

Old things I can reference: _____

_____

_____

_____

Where is the one place I know I can't get any
help? _____

_____

_____

_____

How can I use this? _____

_____

_____

Resources: People

Friends who can help me: _____
_____
_____
_____

Friends of friends who can help me: _____
_____
_____
_____

Family members who can help me: _____
_____
_____
_____

Business associates who can help me: _____
_____
_____
_____

Organizations or associations that can help me: _____
_____
_____
_____

Who will support me? _____

_____

_____

_____

Who can advise me? _____

_____

_____

_____

Who can really help me? _____

_____

_____

_____

People I don't know who can help me: _____

_____

_____

_____

Who is the one person I won't get any help from? __

_____

_____

_____

How can I use even this? _____

_____

_____

_____

Scheduling: Put the "items to do" in chronological order and transfer them to your calendar.

Month:_____

Day:_____ To do: _____

_____   _____

_____   _____

_____   _____

_____   _____

Month:_____

Day:_____ To do: _____

_____   _____

_____   _____

_____   _____

_____   _____

Month:_____

Day:_____ To do: _____

_____   _____

_____   _____

_____   _____

_____   _____

Month:_____

Day:_____ To do: _____

_____   _____

_____   _____

_____   _____

_____   _____

TRUSTING, TIMING, AND YOU

*I am not afraid of tomorrow, for I
have seen yesterday and I love today.*
—*William Allen White*

On the path to making your dreams come true, you're going to meet up with an issue called "trust." Trust, a factor that's at the core of everything, either allows the Magic or keeps it from happening in your life.

What happens when you don't trust is that things get difficult, blocked, stuck, or even fall apart. You start to doubt—first your decision, and eventually everything. You may start to compromise on your dream, and try to manipulate the situation. In your best attempt to control the outcome, you may be the one who unknowingly sabotages your own dream.

The key here is to notice what's going on. When you are aware of the doubts, fears, concerns, and second thoughts, you can stop for a moment and regain some clarity. Start by asking yourself, "What is so?" Better yet, write it out, and write out what you're thinking or telling yourself about "What is so." What stories are you making up that may be disempowering your dream? What are you not trusting and why? How can you

JUST TRUST.

move this obstacle, this mistrust or lack of trust, out of your way? Get clear about what you don't trust and get to the core of it. The heart of where you don't fully have faith can cost you your dream.

Practice letting it go by being more committed to your dream and creating empowering beliefs. Ask yourself what you can do to learn trust, or to help you let go of your lack of trust.

"Letting go" happens when you have clarity about what you want, you've done everything there is to do, and now you can relax. Stop controlling, holding back, fretting, or worrying. Just Trust. Two simpler words may never have been spoken; when it comes to your dream, there is nothing more profound.

Practice "Just Trust." It's a critical component for letting the Magic happen.

> Do you trust yourself and others?
> Do you trust the process, your environment, the universe, the timing, your spiritual nature?
> Do you trust that your dream will come true?

Trust is a giant obstacle for many people. If you don't have it, you'll have to find it, and you'll have to practice trusting yourself above all. Trust the decisions you make, and believe that you're entitled to want your dream and to realize it. Trust comes first; that's what allows the Magic and the extraordinary results to show up.

An effective exercise is to list on a piece of paper the people and things that you do trust and the things that you don't. For example, Stephen, who undertook this exercise, decided the things he trusted included himself, his wife, his minister, one of his co-workers, one of his neighbors, his mother, and his brother. The things in which he didn't have faith included the people outside his immediate environment, and the natural process and timing of things. He also didn't trust that he could have a dream bigger than what already existed in his life.

> # Your dream can be much bigger than your current capacity for dreaming about it.

Being Balanced

One of the ways to develop trust in yourself and the things around you is to keep yourself healthy by being centered and balanced. Feeling good about yourself leads to greater self-confidence, which is one of the places that trust comes from. You are a product of what you eat, how you live, how you rest and how you play, and what you think. All of these things filter into how you feel about yourself and, ultimately, what you allow yourself to trust.

You can work at achieving balance by incorporating some relaxation exercises into your life. The secret is to take it at your own pace, doing activities with which you feel comfortable. Take a few deep, cleansing breaths before you start a new task; closing your eyes and concentrating on your deep breathing will allow you to feel more centered. By "being here and now," you will be in touch with the Magic in your life, and feeling your passion all the time.

This is not about designing a five-year plan for yourself, and then spending another five years figuring out how to control your life and make it happen. It's not about having it all happen right now. It's giving yourself some flow and leeway about what you want, trusting the timing and the process, and being in action in some way each day on the things you love to do.

WHAT I WILL DO TODAY
TO MAKE A DIFFERENCE IN MY LIFE

Starting today, I will do the following for myself:

At home:_____

_____

_____

_____

At work:_____

_____

_____

_____

With others:_____

_____

_____

_____

Alone:_____

_____

_____

_____

_____

The element that's critical to making the timing work in your life is to be present. To be here, right now, enjoying and living your life. Take a look at what matters to you that you're not doing, being, or having. What could you change or create right now that would make a difference? You don't have to restructure your entire life this minute; maybe breathing deeply is all you need right now.

Use the space on page 186 to list the things you will start doing today. These can be simple things: taking an extra five minutes in the morning to stretch and relax, or spending thirty minutes at the end of the day to read the newspaper. Decide what you can do that will keep you centered and balanced.

Magic—In the Flow

Being in the flow means that the timing of your life is working for you, that there's a level of synchronicity where things seem to happen. One of my clients spoke to me of his dream to be featured in the local newspaper. The next day, he called to tell me that the paper, seemingly out of the blue, wanted to interview him.

You can get in sync with the universe when you're not so busy trying to control your life and manipulate everything. Slow down and relax, let go of some of your resistance, and things will seem to happen naturally.

Magic happens when you're living in the flow.

Brian, who was starting a new foundation, devised as one of his projects to get contributions of $25,000 each from ten corporations. While he was working on his strategic plan, he got his first $25,000 from an organization with which he had spoken a long time before. Now he was one-tenth of the way to his goal.

Michelle decided that it was important for her business that she travel to Florida once a month, but she didn't know how she could work it into her budget. The next day, a travel agency called to say that her name had been selected out of a random drawing, and that she'd won six round-trip tickets to Florida. Since then, the trips have proven so fruitful that she is considering relocating to Florida.

Perhaps you have some beliefs about calls that seemingly come "out of the blue." In the case of the man who wanted to appear in the local paper, maybe he was likely to be asked for his views because he was the director of a local association. However, Michelle's experience, winning the round-trip Florida tickets, was pure synchronicity. She had done nothing to put herself in that particular path; it just happened. Brian had planted the seeds, but by his cleaning out the clutter, being in the natural flow, and being willing to have the Magic show up in his life, it did.

This is by no means a trivial component of making your dream come true; the Magic is a gift, and it can show up when you least expect it. Let go of the doubt and fear, and be open to the Magic.

There are other things you can do to increase your sense of Magic and keep yourself centered and balanced. You can take walks in nature, go to the beach and listen to the ocean. Perhaps you will want to give yourself the gift of a extraordinary bath. Take it to the limit: light candles all over the bathroom, play soft music, pour fragrant oils in the tub, and place a bath pillow under your head. Relax, calm yourself, and retreat from worldly concerns. I know city people who go to fountains, sit close, and listen to the rushing water. Visualization exercises, and popularly available meditation tapes, can help you begin to picture and imagine what you want.

When Life Hands You More and More

When the Magic brings you wonderful surprises, as it inevitably will, you might begin to be concerned that you'll have too many things coming at you too fast. After all, if you enroll people in your dream, others will start trying to enroll you in theirs. As more and more possibilities become evident, how will you know when to say yes and when to say no?

Here are some simple questions you can ask yourself to determine whether or not this is right for you:

Is this what I want to do now?
Is this part of my dream?
Is this something I'm passionate or excited about?

You'll know the right answer; it generally comes automatically. You'll know when you're excited about something, or when it seems like a duty. Don't be afraid to affix labels: "This is something I feel I should do." If that's the way you feel, it's a clear indicator that you can let that project go. Other, more passion-provoking opportunities are available.

The possibilities are unlimited as long as you are true to your Life's Purpose.

In fact, the possibilities are unlimited as long as you honor yourself. Follow what has heart and meaning for you. Be willing to say "Yes"; be willing to say "I'll think about it"; and be willing to say "No, thank you!"

BECOMING MAGICAL

One way to get in touch with your magical powers is a technique called imprinting. Close your eyes and get a clear visual image of what you look like as a magical person; are you a wizard, a sorceress, Glinda the Good Witch? Fill in the details of your picture: are you holding a wand, wearing a hat, do you have a big cape around your shoulders? Put your face on the image, or let the image physically walk into you: imprint this magical person inside of you. At the core of you is Magic. Own your magical powers; remember who you are. Magic is not something that you just let into your life once in a while. *Magic is your essence.*

DARE TO DREAM BIG

*Never doubt that a small group of thoughtful,
committed citizens can change the world;
indeed it's the only thing that ever has.*
—*Margaret Mead*

Since page 1, we've focused on you and your dream; now we're going to turn a corner. The goal of this chapter is to inspire you to dream bigger—to go beyond what you've chosen so far.

If you want to have a life that's filled with passion, I encourage you to create a project that's "Bigger than Your Life." This project is "A Big One," one you don't know how to accomplish, but one that comes from your passion.

Once you're clear about what you're committed to, incredible resources, possibilities, and Magic will show up to help you. Although it may not be completed during your lifetime, it will allow you to play an extraordinary game. You will definitely feel passion.

Imagine having the dream of a world that works, or of creating heaven on earth in your own special way. There have been many big dreamers before you—Kennedy, King, Gandhi—but there are also everyday people who absolutely can make a contribution to the world. Pursuing your Big Dream is not only about doing what you say or what you want; it's actually being and becoming a different kind of person.

Where do you begin? In what area are you committed to making a difference? Are you committed to a planet that's clean and healthy? A man I know has a Big Dream to ensure that the rain forest is still in existence when his children's children are grown. Maybe your interest is in the area of health and medicine. How about a cure for cancer or AIDS in your lifetime? Or

I have not the shadow of a
doubt that any man or
woman can achieve what I have,
if he or she would make the
same effort and cultivate
the same hope and faith.

What is faith if it is not
translated into action?

—Mahatma Gandhi

maybe your dream, to have more breathable air, can encompass both health and environmental issues. Perhaps your contribution will be in the area of media or communications.

As I mentioned, my Big Dream is to change the way people think about dreams. I want people to stop thinking about dreams in the negative, that dreams are something they can't have. Instead, I want people to think, "Dream? By when?" and start applying dates to their dreams.

Whatever your Big Dream is, this is an opportunity for you to get into action on it. You might be asking what difference you can make if you're only one individual. The Real People stories in this chapter are about individuals who made a major contribution to society. Among them is the story of Anselm, an ordinary man who made a big difference by touching many lives globally with the projects he produced. He was only one individual, but he had a unique and special dream: to end world hunger.

If you are not the kind of person who can start a Soviet-American Citizens Summit or a Make a Wish Foundation, perhaps you are the type who can volunteer at such an organization. Look around. Start with what you're passionate about, what matters to you, what moves you. Talk with people who are already involved and learn how you can participate. Make a contribution; that's the way to Dare to Dream Big. Make a promise and then take action to fulfill your promise; that's what your life is about.

How can you get into action? Mark your calendar; talk to someone; listen for a request; ask how you can help. As you're watching television or reading the newspaper, notice what moves you, angers you, turns you on and touches your heart. That's a good place to begin.

The critical thing is to begin. One thing will lead to another. You'll know when it feels right, and the personal feeling of satisfaction and fulfillment will be beyond description. Perhaps all we want from our lives is to make a difference. This is one way to do it: Dare to Dream Big.

We are not here
to do what has
already been done.
—Robert Henri

REAL PEOPLE: ANSELM ROTHSCHILD

Anselm Rothschild, a friend, was committed to ending hunger in the world, and he dedicated his life to doing it. He chose to pursue his dream by composing music and producing events that promoted global peace and an end to hunger.

During the 1960s, Anselm organized the Freedom from Hunger Foundation's first walkathon, which became the prototype for fund-raising walkathons across the country. He didn't stop there, however. While Anselm had lots of credits and credentials, he is probably best remembered as the head writer and coordinating producer of the educational components of the "LiveAid" telecast.

Anselm was a man who followed his dream. I speak about him in the past tense because, unfortunately, he died before he reached forty. But what a life he lived.

He was indeed an extraordinary man, and he wrote a wonderful song that sums up much of what I've said in this book. It's called "Remember to Remember," and you will find the lyrics on page 195.

Although he wasn't able to end world hunger by the time he died, his contribution made a specific and measurable difference to billions of people. Anselm's message raised awareness of the problem to a new level through "LiveAid," which was broadcast worldwide to 160 countries and seen by three billion people.

REAL PEOPLE: RAMA AND BARBARA

Years ago, I had the honor of co-producing the Soviet-American Citizens Summit Awards ceremony. In the course of my work on that project, I met Rama Vernon and Barbara Marx Hubbard, special individuals who had founded the Soviet-American Citizens Summit.

Rama was an average woman, a homemaker who was cred-

REMEMBER TO REMEMBER

Remember to remember,
It will light your heart each day,
It will help you on your way,
And it's more than just a saying so you know.

Remember to remember,
That is all you have to do,
And the truth will see you through
Even when all has darkened around you.

Who you said you are was brighter than a star,
Even though your dreams were dashed and knocked
  about,
You were still that dream under everything you doubt.

Remember to remember
How you said you wanted to be;
It will set and keep you free;
It will heal your wounds, caress your face with love.

Remember to remember,
If it's all you ever do,
And the truth will see you through;
You will hear God sing to you forever.

Who you said you are was brighter than a star,
Even though your dreams were dashed and knocked
  about,
You were still that dream under everything you doubt.

Remember to remember,
If it's all you ever do,
And the truth will see you through;
You will hear God sing to you forever.

© Anselm Rothschild

ited by the president of the Soviet Peace Commission with "coming out of her kitchen" and bravely leading a group of committed Americans to the Soviet Union with the objective of creating a dialogue. Out of Rama's vision and her dream came the Citizens Summit, through which thousands of people from all over the world gathered to partner on various projects.

Rama's and Barbara's vision came long before it was in vogue to travel to the Soviet Union. The organization lives on today, having set the tone for relationships among all the citizens of the world.

REAL PEOPLE: THE VOLUNTEERS OF THE MAKE A WISH FOUNDATION

The Make a Wish Foundation is a nonprofit, volunteer organization whose sole aim is to grant the wishes of children under the age of eighteen who are suffering from life-threatening illnesses. The foundation was started in 1980, when a dying youngster's dream to become a state trooper was granted. Since then, more than ten thousand children across the United States have had their dreams come true, thanks to the Make a Wish Foundation.

Granting a sick child's special wish provides a joyful and meaningful experience that benefits both the child and the family. Whether a child wishes to take a hot air balloon ride, visit

---

Everyday, ordinary
people launch dreams
bigger than themselves.

---

a favorite sports hero, or spend time at Disney World, the Make a Wish Foundation does everything possible to ensure that the wish becomes a reality.

The foundation depends completely on financial donations and on its volunteers' contributions of time. Those who elect to give of their energy are remarkable individuals, making the dreams of ailing children come true while satisfying their own desire to make a difference.

> # Dreams bigger than your life start the same as all dreams.

CHAPTER EIGHTEEN

WORDS FOR MAKING YOUR DREAMS COME TRUE: A NEW WAY OF SPEAKING

*To speak of "mere words" is much
like speaking of "mere dynamite."*
—C. J. Ducasse

The following words and definitions, as used in this book, are also used regularly by people who make their dreams come true. Think of these terms as a new way of speaking your dream, to bring the Magic into your life.

Accomplishment, something that you have done, succeeded in, or completed in the past that you are proud of; something that you're passionate about.

Acknowledge, to recognize someone or something.

Action, to move from one point to another; to be in motion; a dynamic movement forward.

Alignment, when everything is arranged in a way that works and supports the whole.

Balance, equal on all sides; the outcome is a sense of well-being and ease.

Belief, an opinion or judgment you hold to be true.

Clarity, focus; a clear way of seeing something.

Coach, a person who is committed to your being a champion.

Completion, when something is whole; has integrity; all the pieces are there.

Conversation, a way of communicating and interacting with another person.

Design, to make something happen intentionally.

Devise, to plan; to create a plan of action.

Dream, a fond hope and a plan for accomplishing it.

Dream architect, someone who helps other people accomplish their dreams by helping them get clear about what they want, by helping them to design a blueprint for achieving their dreams, and by helping them make their dreams come true.

Dream scheme, a plan of action for getting what you want.

Dynamic, an energetic force that is intense, exuberant, unstoppable, in motion, full speed ahead, moving forward.

Energy, a force; a potential; the ability to move.

Enrollment, sharing your dream in such a way that other people get excited.

Expressing, a way of communicating; conversing, relating, telling, declaring, imparting information to others.

Focus, an ability to see things clearly using different perspectives.

Fun, amusement, mirth, gaiety.

Happy, lightness, enjoyment, pleasurable, feeling good.

Harmony, when all things work together in unison.

Holograph, the wholeness of an item; three-dimensional; a new way of looking at something.

Intention, focus; direction.

Love, your first priority; a way of being; that which has deep meaning and significance for you.

Magic, producing extraordinary results.

Measurable, something that can be evaluated using preset criteria.

Movement, relocation of something from one place to another.

Nightmares, your worst dreams; dreams turned bad; negative ideas or concerns; fears; visions you may have when you're sleeping.

Opportunities, ways of accomplishing something.

Participation, involvement; making something happen.

Partnership, being in a relationship with people who can help you make your dreams come true.

Passion, feeling turned on, energized, excited, enthusiastic; going full out, aligning mind, body, heart.

Play, to engage in, undertake, perform.

Possibility, the belief that anything and everything can happen; a powerful force.

Power, a form of energy, such as owning your own power; energetic movement from A to B; also a form of empowerment.

Project, a unit of measure for accomplishing something; an accomplishment with a specific, measurable result; the way to bring your dreams into tangible form.

Purpose, who you are in the world; work that you have chosen to do in the world; where passion comes from; what turns you on.

Relationship, a way of being with another person or other people or things.

Resources, tools that are available to help you make your dreams come true, including people, places, things, and you.

Result, an accomplishment; something complete and whole that stands alone; something that can be identified and measured.

Schedule, to put something on your calendar; to assign a date by which something will happen.

Scheme, a plan of action.

Specific, an individual unit that is identifiable in time and space.

Strategy, a way of doing something; the "how" of getting something accomplished.

Success, a self-defined way of being, the outcome of which is a feeling of joy.

Tactics, the specific items to get you into action on making your dream come true.

Unlimited, no limitations on what you want to accomplish.

Unstoppable, to keep going, no matter what happens.

Values, a way of being; a way of living your life.

Vision, a clear picture of what you want to accomplish or create.

Vitality, a level of energy and usefulness that one may have when living life on purpose.

Way of being, the expression of someone living their life in passion.

Way of living, unlimited; no restrictions; anything goes.

Whole, something that is, or someone that is, complete and intact and has all the pieces.

Work, an expression of who you are in the world.

CHAPTER NINETEEN

EPILOGUE: THE BEGINNING

Some people believe that only God can make
dreams come true. I believe that we are
co-creators in designing the plan of our lives.
—Marcia Wieder

Although this is the last chapter of the book, it is only the beginning for you. Remember the story of co-creating in chapter 3? You are the creator of the life you want to live, and you can devise dreams that will come true, picket fence and all.

Remember that the formula is simple:

1. Get clear about what you want to create,
2. Remove the obstacles, and
3. Allow the Magic to happen or Design the Strategies to get there.

Standing in your Purpose and moving up the Passion Pyramid, you can see your dreams in crystal clarity and commit to having them. Use your resources, the ones you know about right now and the ones you can make available to yourself. Allow yourself to be imaginative and inventive, to create projects that will move you forward.

Design your internal and external environments so that they are supportive of your dreams and projects and will make your dreams come true. Trust the process, the synchronicity in the universe, and, most of all, trust yourself. You are, and you can be, as imaginative and resourceful as you need to be; get in action to live the life you love.

Share your dream with others; the process will help you enroll people who will want to contribute time and energy to fulfilling your dream. When you can envision it in its entirety, you will be able to speak your dream in a way that generates excitement and enthusiasm. The eagerness you engender in others will come back to you a thousandfold in heightened motivation to make your dreams come true.

Be unstoppable. You can have the life you want, the one that works for you. The possibilities are all waiting for you to let them happen, to produce extraordinary results, to make your life the magical experience it was meant to be.

Making Your Dreams Come True® Cards

Based on Marcia Wieder's book, *Making Your Dreams Come True*, these 40 daily affirmation cards guide you toward your goals. Whimsical illustrations of the magical wizards, Merlin and Merinda, help you discover and achieve the life you want!

Live Powerfully

Follow Your Heart

Share the Dream

(shown smaller than actual size)

ONLY
$12.98

includes deluxe drawstring pouch

To order by phone call: **(800) 334-8232**

To order by mail send to: MasterMedia Ltd.
17 E. 89th Street
New York, NY 10128

QTY.	DESCRIPTION	PRICE	TOTAL
	Making Your Dreams Come True Cards	$12.98 each	
	☐ Check or money order payable to **MasterMedia Ltd.**	SHIPPING/ HANDLING	$3.00
	☐ Visa ☐ Mastercard	TOTAL DUE	

Please include credit card number, expiration date and signature with charge orders.

Card No.: ☐☐☐☐☐☐☐☐☐☐☐☐☐   Exp. Date: ☐☐ / ☐☐

Signature _____

Ship to:

Name _____

Street _____

City _____   State _____   Zip _____

Phone: Day (   )   Eve (   ) _____

ABOUT THE AUTHOR

Marcia Wieder is living proof that we can and do create our own reality. She has mastered doing what she says: making her own dreams come true and living a life of passion.

With her television background and marketing expertise, Marcia became fascinated with the concept of "vision" and developing the ability to "speak things into being." As a professional speaker, her spirit and presence fill any room. She produces dynamic results with her corporate clients and business associates worldwide.

Marcia's energetic presentation is balanced with tangible, usable tips and techniques for creating a life that works, a life filled with joy, balance, and dreams come true. Marcia's speeches seem to blend brand-new information with ideas that are thousands of years old. A session with Marcia has been described as "absolutely filled with unlimited possibilities."

Taking a systematic approach, Marcia has designed a step-by-step process for making dreams come true. After speaking with Marcia, people who claim to have forgotten their dream remember it; and those who are clear about their dream become immersed in the specifics of how to make it come true.

Additional copies of *Making Your Dreams Come True* may be ordered by sending a check for $9.95 (please add the following for postage and handling: $2.00 for the first copy, $1.00 for each added copy) to:

MasterMedia Limited
17 East 89th Street
New York, NY 10128
(212) 260-5600
(800) 334-8232
fax: (212) 546-7638

The author is available for workshops, seminars, and speeches. Please contact MasterMedia's Speakers' Bureau for availability and fee arrangements. Call Tony Colao at (800) 4-LECTUR; fax: (908) 359-1647.

OTHER MASTERMEDIA
BOOKS

To order MasterMedia books, either visit your local bookstore or call (800) 334-8232.

THE PREGNANCY AND MOTHERHOOD DIARY: Planning the First Year of Your Second Career, by Susan Schiffer Stautberg, is the first and only undated appointment diary that shows how to manage pregnancy and career. ($12.95 spiral-bound)

CITIES OF OPPORTUNITY: Finding the Best Place to Work, Live and Prosper in the 1990's and Beyond, by Dr. John Tepper Marlin, explores the job and living options for the next decade and into the next century. This consumer guide and handbook, written by one of the world's experts on cities, selects and features forty-six American cities and metropolitan areas. ($13.95 paper, $24.95 cloth)

THE DOLLARS AND SENSE OF DIVORCE, by Dr. Judith Briles, is the first book to combine practical tips on overcoming the legal hurdles by planning finances before, during, and after divorce. ($10.95 paper)

OUT THE ORGANIZATION: New Career Opportunities for the 1990's, by Robert and Madeleine Swain, is written for the millions of Americans whose jobs are no longer safe, whose companies are not loyal, and who face futures of uncertainty. It gives advice on finding a new job or starting your own business. ($12.95 paper)

AGING PARENTS AND YOU: A Complete Handbook to Help You Help Your Elders Maintain a Healthy, Productive and Independent Life, by Eugenia Anderson-Ellis, is a complete guide to providing care to aging relatives. It gives practical advice and resources to the adults who are helping their elders lead productive and independent lives. Revised and updated. ($9.95 paper)

CRITICISM IN YOUR LIFE: How to Give It, How to Take It, How to Make It Work for You, by Dr. Deborah Bright, offers practical advice, in an upbeat, readable, and realistic fashion, for turning criticism into control. Charts and diagrams guide the reader into managing criticism from bosses, spouses, children, friends, neighbors, in-laws, and business relations. ($17.95 cloth)

BEYOND SUCCESS: How Volunteer Service Can Help You Begin Making a Life Instead of Just a Living, by John F. Raynolds III and Eleanor Raynolds, C.B.E., is a unique how-to book targeted at business and professional people considering volunteer work, senior citizens who wish to fill leisure time meaningfully, and students trying out various career options. The book is filled with interviews with celebrities, CEOs, and average citizens who talk about the benefits of service work. ($19.95 cloth)

MANAGING IT ALL: Time-Saving Ideas for Career, Family, Relationships, and Self, by Beverly Benz Treuille and Susan Schiffer Stautberg, is written for women who are juggling careers and families. Over two hundred career women (ranging from a TV anchorwoman to an investment banker) were interviewed. The book contains many humorous anecdotes on saving time and improving the quality of life for self and family. ($9.95 paper)

YOUR HEALTHY BODY, YOUR HEALTHY LIFE: How to Take Control of Your Medical Destiny, by Donald B. Louria, M.D., provides precise advice and strategies that will help you to live a long and healthy life. Learn also about nutrition, exercise, vitamins, and medication, as well as how to control risk factors for major diseases. Revised and updated. ($12.95 paper)

THE CONFIDENCE FACTOR: How Self-Esteem Can Change Your Life, by Dr. Judith Briles, is based on a nationwide survey of six thousand men and women. Briles explores why women so often feel a lack of self-confidence and have a poor opinion of themselves. She offers step-by-step advice on becoming the person you want to be. ($9.95 paper, $18.95 cloth)

THE SOLUTION TO POLLUTION: 101 Things You Can Do to Clean Up Your Environment, by Laurence Sombke, offers step-by-step techniques on how to conserve more energy, start a recycling center, choose biodegradable products, and even proceed with individual environmental cleanup projects. ($7.95 paper)

TAKING CONTROL OF YOUR LIFE: The Secrets of Successful Enterprising Women, by Gail Blanke and Kathleen Walas, is based on the authors' professional experience with Avon Products' Women of Enterprise Awards, given each year to outstanding women entrepreneurs. The authors offer a specific plan to help you gain control over your life, and include business tips and quizzes as well as beauty and lifestyle information. ($17.95 cloth)

SIDE-BY-SIDE STRATEGIES: How Two-Career Couples Can Thrive in the Nineties, by Jane Hershey Cuozzo and S. Diane Graham, describes how two-career couples can learn the difference between competing with a spouse and becoming a supportive power partner. Published in hardcover as *Power Partners.* ($10.95 paper, $19.95 cloth)

DARE TO CONFRONT! How to Intervene When Someone You Care About Has an Alcohol or Drug Problem, by Bob Wright and Deborah George Wright, shows the reader how to use the step-by-step methods of professional interventionists to motivate drug-dependent people to accept the help they need. ($17.95 cloth)

WORK WITH ME! How to Make the Most of Office Support Staff, by Betsy Lazary, shows you how to find, train, and nurture the "perfect" assistant and how to best utilize your support staff professionals. ($9.95 paper)

MANN FOR ALL SEASONS: Wit and Wisdom from The Washington Post*'s Judy Mann,* by Judy Mann, shows the columnist at her best as she writes about women, families, and the impact and politics of the women's revolution. ($9.95 paper, $19.95 cloth)

THE SOLUTION TO POLLUTION IN THE WORKPLACE, by Laurence Sombke, Terry M. Robertson and Elliot M. Kaplan, supplies employees with everything they need to know about cleaning up their workspace, including recycling, using energy efficiently, conserving water and buying recycled products and nontoxic supplies. ($9.95 paper)

THE ENVIRONMENTAL GARDENER: The Solution to Pollution for Lawns and Gardens, by Laurence Sombke, focuses on what each of us can do to protect our endangered plant life. A practical sourcebook and shopping guide. ($8.95 paper)

THE LOYALTY FACTOR: Building Trust in Today's Workplace, by Carol Kinsey Goman, Ph.D., offers techniques for restoring commitment and loyalty in the workplace. ($9.95 paper)

DARE TO CHANGE YOUR JOB—AND YOUR LIFE, by Carole Kanchier, Ph.D., provides a look at career growth and development throughout the life cycle. ($9.95 paper)

MISS AMERICA: In Pursuit of the Crown, by Ann-Marie Bivans, is an authorized guidebook to the Pageant, containing eyewitness accounts, complete historical data, and a realistic look at the trials and triumphs of the potential Miss Americas. ($19.95 paper, $27.50 cloth; b & w and color photos)

POSITIVELY OUTRAGEOUS SERVICE: New and Easy Ways to Win Customers for Life, by T. Scott Gross, identifies what the consumers of the nineties really want and how businesses can develop effective marketing strategies to answer those needs. ($14.95 paper)

BREATHING SPACE: Living and Working at a Comfortable Pace in a Sped-Up Society, by Jeff Davidson, helps readers to handle information and activity overload, and gain greater control over their lives. ($10.95 paper)

TWENTYSOMETHING: Managing and Motivating Today's New Work Force, by Lawrence J. Bradford, Ph.D., and Claire Raines, M.A., examines the work orientation of the younger generation, offering managers in businesses of all kinds a practical guide to better understand and supervise their young employees. ($22.95 cloth)

REAL LIFE 101: The Graduate's Guide to Survival, by Susan Kleinman, supplies welcome advice to those facing "real life" for the first time, focusing on work, money, health, and how to deal with freedom and responsibility. ($9.95 paper)

BALANCING ACTS! Juggling Love, Work, Family, and Recreation, by Susan Schiffer Stautberg and Marcia L. Worthing, provides strategies to achieve a balanced life by reordering priorities and setting realistic goals. ($12.95 paper)

REAL BEAUTY . . . REAL WOMEN: A Handbook for Making the Best of Your Own Good Looks, by Kathleen Walas, International Beauty and Fashion Director of Avon Products, offers expert advice on beauty and fashion to women of all ages and ethnic backgrounds. ($19.50 paper; in full color)

THE LIVING HEART BRAND NAME SHOPPER'S GUIDE (Revised and Updated), by Michael E. DeBakey, M.D., Antonio M. Gotto, Jr., M.D., D.Phil., Lynne W. Scott, M.A., R.D./L.D., and John P. Foreyt, Ph.D., lists brand-name supermarket products that are low in fat, saturated fatty acids, and cholesterol. ($14.95 paper)

MANAGING YOUR CHILD'S DIABETES, by Robert Wood Johnson IV, Sale Johnson, Casey Johnson, and Susan Kleinman, brings help to families trying to understand diabetes and control its effects. ($10.95 paper)

STEP FORWARD: Sexual Harassment in the Workplace, What You Need to Know, by Susan L. Webb, presents the facts for identifying the tell-tale signs of sexual harassment on the job, and how to deal with it. ($9.95 paper)

A TEEN'S GUIDE TO BUSINESS: The Secrets to a Successful Enterprise, by Linda Menzies, Oren S. Jenkins, and Rickell R. Fisher, provides solid information about starting a business or working for one. ($7.95 paper)

GLORIOUS ROOTS: Recipes for Healthy, Tasty Vegetables, by Laurence Sombke, celebrates the taste, texture, and versatility of root vegetables. Contains recipes for appetizers, soups, stews, and baked, boiled, and stir-fried dishes—even desserts. ($12.95 paper)

THE OUTDOOR WOMAN: A Handbook to Adventure, by Patricia Hubbard and Stan Wass, details the lives of adventurous outdoor women and offers their ideas on how you can incorporate exciting outdoor experiences into your life. ($14.95 paper; with photos)

FLIGHT PLAN FOR LIVING: The Art of Self-Encouragement, by Patrick O'Dooley, is a life-guide organized like a pilot's flight checklist, which ensures you'll be flying "clear on top" throughout your life. ($17.95 cloth)

HOW TO GET WHAT YOU WANT FROM ALMOST ANYBODY, by T. Scott Gross, shows how to get great service, negotiate better prices, and always get what you pay for. ($9.95 paper)

TEAMBUILT: Making Teamwork Work, by Mark Sanborn, teaches business how to improve productivity, without increasing resources or expenses, by building teamwork among employers. ($19.95 cloth)

THE BIG APPLE BUSINESS AND PLEASURE GUIDE: 501 Ways to Work Smarter, Play Harder, and Live Better in New York City, by Muriel Siebert and Susan Kleinman, offers visitors and New Yorkers alike advice on how to do business in the city as well as how to enjoy its attractions. ($9.95 paper)

FINANCIAL SAVVY FOR WOMEN: A Money Book for Women of All Ages, by Dr. Judith Briles, provides a critical and in-depth look at financial structures and tools any woman wanting to achieve total independence can use. ($14.95 paper)

MIND YOUR OWN BUSINESS: And Keep It in the Family, by Marcy Syms, COO of Syms Corporation, is an effective guide for any organization, small or large, facing what is documented to be the toughest step in managing a family business—making the transition to the new generation. ($18.95 cloth)

KIDS WHO MAKE A DIFFERENCE, by Joyce M. Roché and Marie Rodriguez, with Phyllis Schneider, is a surprising and inspiring document of some of today's toughest challenges being met—by teenagers and kids! Their courage and creativity allowed them to find practical solutions. ($8.95 paper; with photos)

ROSEY GRIER'S ALL-AMERICAN HEROS: Multicultural Success Stories, by Roosevelt "Rosey" Grier, is a wonderful collection of personal histories, told in their own words by prominent African-Americans, Latins, Asians, and native Americans; all tell of the people in their lives and choices they made in achieving public acclaim and personal success. ($9.95 paper; with portrait photos)

OFFICE BIOLOGY: Why Tuesday Is the Most Productive Day and Other Relevant Facts for Survival in the Workplace, by Edith Weiner and Arnold Brown, teaches how in the nineties and beyond we will be expected to work smarter, take better control of our health, adapt to advancing technology, and improve our lives in ways that are not too costly or resource-intensive. ($21.95 cloth)

ON TARGET: Enhance Your Life and Ensure Your Success, by Jeri Sedlar and Rick Miners, is a neatly woven tapestry of insights on career and life issues gathered from audiences across the country. This feedback has been crystallized into a highly readable guidebook for exploring who you are and how to go about getting what you want from your career and your life. ($11.95 paper)

SOMEONE ELSE'S SON, by Alan A. Winter, explores the parent-child bond in a contemporary story of lost identities, family secrets, and relationships gone awry. Eighteen years after bringing their first son home from the hospital, Trish and Brad Hunter discover that they are not his natural parents. Torn between their love for their son, Phillip, and the question of whether they should help him search for his biological parents, the couple must also struggle with the issue of their own biological son. Who is he—and do his parents know that their baby was switched at birth? ($18.95 cloth)

STRAIGHT TALK ON WOMEN'S HEALTH: How to Get the Health Care You Deserve, by Janice Teal, Ph.D., and Phyllis Schneider, is destined to become a health-care bible for women concerned about their bodies and their future health. Well-researched but devoid of confusing medical jargon, this handbook offers access to a wealth of resources, with a bibliography of health-related books and contact lists of organizations, healthlines, and women's medical centers. ($14.95 paper)

THE STEPPARENT CHALLENGE: A Primer for Making It Work, by Stephen J. Williams, Ph.D., shares firsthand experience and insights into the many aspects of dealing with step relationships—from financial issues to lifestyle changes to differences in race or religion that affect the whole family. Peppered with personal accounts and useful tips, this volume is must reading for anyone who is a stepparent, about to become one, or planning to bring children to a second or subsequent marriage. ($13.95 paper)

PAIN RELIEF! How to Say No to Acute, Chronic, and Cancer Pain, by Dr. Jane Cowles, offers a step-by-step plan for assessing pain and communicating it to your doctor, and explains the importance of having a pain plan before undergoing any medical or surgical treatment. This landmark book includes ''The Pain Patient's Bill of Rights'' and a reusable pain assessment chart designed to help patients and their families make informed decisions. ($22.95 cloth)

WHAT KIDS LIKE TO DO, by Edward Stautberg, Gail Wubbenhorst, Atiya Easterling, and Phyllis Schneider, is a handy guidebook for parents, grand-parents, and baby-sitters who are searching for activities that kids *really* enjoy. Written by kids for kids, this easy-to-read, generously illustrated primer can teach families how to make every day more fun. ($7.95 paper)

The
"MAKING YOUR DREAMS COME TRUE"
Series
Presentations designed to get you "IN ACTION"

MOTIVATION
- Passion and Productivity
- Creating a Company that Works!
- Dare to Dream Big: Using Your Resources to Make a Difference

SALES
- A Dream Come True: Making Great Money
  Doing What You Love
- Magic: Producing Extraordinary Results
- Passion: Access to an Easy Sale

TIME MANAGEMENT
- The Impossible Dream—Strategies for a Balanced Life
- Dreamschemes—A Blueprint for Getting There. Anywhere
- Extra Energy and Extra Time—Am I Dreaming?

PERSONAL DEVELOPMENT
- Breakthrough Thinking: Living from Your Passion vs.
  Your Calendar
- Blasting Barriers and Beliefs and Being Unstoppable
- Living Your Dream Life: Yes, You Can Still Have It All

WORKPLACE/TEAM BUILDING
- Reigniting Passion in the Workplace and Your Life
- Mapping Your Leadership Vision
- The Dream Team: Playing with Winners to Win

For information on booking Marcia for your next conference,
please call Tony Colao at (800) 4-LECTUR